CONTRACTS
OF
EMPLOYMENT

AUSTRALIA AND NEW ZEALAND
The Law Book Company Ltd.
Sydney : Melbourne : Brisbane : Perth

CANADA
The Carswell Company Ltd.
Toronto : Calgary : Vancouver : Ottawa

INDIA
N. M. Tripathi Private Ltd.
Bombay
and
Eastern Law House Private Ltd.
Calcutta

M.P.P. House
Bangalore

ISRAEL
Steimatzky's Agency Ltd.
Jerusalem : Tel Aviv : Haifa

PAKISTAN
Pakistan Law House
Karachi

CONTRACTS
OF
EMPLOYMENT

BY

NEIL FAGAN

LONDON
SWEET & MAXWELL
1990

Published in 1990 by
Sweet & Maxwell Limited, of
South Quay Plaza,
183 Marsh Wall, London E14 9FT
Phototypeset by
LBJ Enterprises Limited
Chilcompton, Somerset
and printed in Great Britain by
Butler and Tanner Limited
Frome, Somerset

British Library Cataloguing in Publication Data
Fagan, Neil
    Contracts of Employment
    1. Great Britain. Employment. Contracts. Law
    I. Title
    344.10624

ISBN 0–421–41910–5

ACKNOWLEDGEMENT

I would like to acknowledge the great help and encouragement I have had from my secretary, Marian Stiff, who has also been responsible for typing and correcting the manuscript. I would also like to thank the members of the employment and pensions group at Lovell White Durrant who have given me enormous help in the production of material for the book, in particular, and in no particular order, Elizabeth Slattery, Barbara Morris, Nicholas Robertson, John Pearson, Naomi Feinstein and last, but not least, Andrew Wiliamson who was forced to read and comment, with his usual verve and clarity, on some of the chapters of the book. A special thank you also to Simon Richardson.

CONTENTS

CONTENTS

CONTENTS

TABLE OF CASES

TABLE OF CASES

TABLE OF CASES

TABLE OF CASES

TABLE OF CASES

TABLE OF CASES

xvi

TABLE OF CASES

TABLE OF CASES

TABLE OF STATUTES

TABLE OF STATUTES

TABLE OF STATUTORY INSTRUMENTS

CONTRACTS OF EMPLOYMENT

Introduction

This book is about contracts of employment and it is hoped that it will provide a handy reference book for all the up to date case law on contracts of employment in one volume. We have seen a plethora of material from Parliament and from the courts and, indeed, textbook writers, dealing with industrial relations issues, trades unions, strikes, ballots and so forth. There are, however, a large number of people who are regularly involved in the day to day creation and termination of contracts of employment. This is the very essence of legal work in the employment field and it has been slightly neglected by writers in favour of the rather more high profile industrial relations activities of the last 10 or 15 years.

There are commonly held misconceptions about contracts of employment. Every person who works for someone else, whether that someone else be an individual, company, partnership or other entity, is in a contractual relationship with that person, whether there is total silence as to the terms of that relationship and whether or not there is anything in writing. The common law has for years recognised certain implied terms to fill any lacuna in the written contract and practitioners in the field still refer to cases which mark important steps in the development of the implied duties and obligations of employer and employee. See *Hivac Comma Ltd.* v. *Park Royal Scientific Instruments Ltd.*,[1] *Wessex Dairies* v. *Smith*,[2] *British Syphon Co. Ltd.* v. *Homewood*,[3] *Bell* v. *Lever Bros.*[4] References made to these authorities and others can be found in Chapter 3 which deals with implied terms.

Since the landmark Industrial Relations Act 1971 there have been the following major statutes which have an impact on the employment relationship and, therefore, on the contract of employment:

---

[1] [1946] Ch. 169.
[2] [1935] 2 K.B. 80.
[3] [1956] 2 A.E.R. 897.
[4] [1932] A.C. 161.

CONTRACTS OF EMPLOYMENT

The Equal Pay Act 1970 (although predating the 1971 Act, it took effect thereafter)
European Communities Act 1972
Trade Union and Labour Relations Act 1974
Rehabilitation of Offenders Act 1974
Sex Discrimination Act 1975
Employment Protection Act 1974
Employment Protection Act 1975
Trade Union and Labour Relations (Amendment) Act 1976
Race Relations Act 1976
Employment Protection (Consolidation) Act 1978
Employment Act 1980
Social Security and Housing Benefits Act 1982
Employment Act 1982
Trade Union Act 1984
Wages Act 1986
Sex Discrimination Act 1986
Social Security Act 1986
Employment Act 1988

This tremendous pace of legislative change has resulted in something of a "minefield" for practitioners in the field. This book tries to take a fresh look at how all this legislation has affected the contract of employment and how the courts and Industrial Tribunals have reacted to it by referring to a large number of recent cases.

The contract of employment is like no other type of contract, mainly because it directly affects the relationship between people in the very core of their lives: their working environment. It is trite to say that we spend more time at work than in any other facet of our lives and the terms and conditions that affect that part of our lives are, or at least should be, of considerable significance to us. Some call the employment contract a "dynamic" one in that it is constantly developing by reason of changing work practices and the like. Some would say that it is really not necessary to reduce all these matters to writing because if the relationship works it will work in any event and if it does not then it is as well that it should end.

What it is hoped this book will provide is a straightforward and practical guide to the current state of the law in relation to contracts of employment, an analysis of how the contract changes without necessarily being rewritten, the effect of the statutory overlay onto freely negotiated terms and conditions and lastly the important impact of European legislation on domestic legislation and contracts of employment.

CHAPTER 1

THE CONTRACT OF EMPLOYMENT

Introduction

The basic question to start with is whether or not someone works under **1.1**
a contract of employment. This is a legal matter. If there is a written
contract the question of whether or not it is a contract for service or for
the provision of services is also one of law. An individual could provide
services exactly the same as those under a contract of employment but
through his own company so that the company contracts with the
"employer" to provide the services of the employee. However, the
provision of services is distinguished in the normal way from a contract
of service. As Lord Denning has said:

> "under a contract of service, a man is employed as part of the business
> and his work is done as an integral part of the business; whereas under a
> contract for services his work, though done for the business, is not
> integrated into it."[1]

Where the contract is not in written form whether or not an employment
contract exists is a question of fact, not law. There is a fairly fine
distinction between the question of law, whether someone works under
a contract of employment and whether or not a contract of employment
exists but that distinction can be found in two cases, *Davies* v.
Presbyterian Church of Wales[2] and *Global Plant Ltd.* v. *Secretary of*

---

[1] See *C. Stevenson Jordan & Harrison Ltd.* v. *MacDonald and Evans* [1952] 1 T.L.R. 101
(C.A.).
[2] [1986] I.R.L.R. 194, (H.L.).

3

State of Social Services.[3] Employers should avoid points such as these and disputes on these matters by:

- ensuring that contracts of employment for their employees are in writing,
- stating clearly and concisely what the terms of the employment are,
- indicating specifically by reference any other documents which are deemed to be incorporated in the employment contract;
- providing for the employee to acknowledge receipt of all relevant documents, or alternatively to have access thereto and above all by ensuring that the employee is bound by such terms.

Creation of the Contract

1.2 If the employer wishes to create a contract of employment and not a contract for the provision of services, the basic contractual capacity of the parties is regulated by the usual rules of contract. A minor is only bound by a contract if it is for his benefit, looked at as a whole in the light of the circumstances when it was made,[4] There are no special rules as to the form of the contract. Very often drafters of contracts will use the statutory written particulars required under section 1 of the Employment Protection (Consolidation) Act 1978 ("E.P.C.A.") referred to below as a basic framework and there are many standard printed forms which follow such a framework.

Offer and Acceptance

1.3 A contract of employment is, therefore, created by the simple offer of employment subsequently accepted. There have been a number of occasions where employers have been caught out by offering employment to an individual, the offer has been accepted, and subsequently the employer finds out that there is some reason why they do not want to continue to take the person on. Very often an assumption is made that the employer can simply disengage. A contract has, however, been

---

[3] [1971] 1 Q.B. 139.
[4] *Doyle* v. *White City Stadium Ltd.* [1935] 1 K.B. 110.

created and has to be terminated. If the terms of the offer and acceptance included any provision as to notice, then notice will, on the face of it, have to be given subject to any obligation to mitigate.

Mitigation is the legal concept pursuant to which people who have suffered loss by reason of a breach of contract are obliged to minimise that loss by, in the case of employment, seeking alternative employment. The money earned from fresh employment goes to "mitigate" the loss suffered by reason of the breach of the first employment. It is not even necessary for the offer to be made directly to the offeree. In *Marsden & Others* v. *Fairey Stainless Steel Ltd.*[5] where the employee knew of the contents of a letter containing an offer of re-engagement after a strike dismissal and he believed it to be applicable to him, this constituted an effective offer made to him. There is no requirement under statute that an offer should be written or made directly to the offeree. Admittedly this was an offer of re-engagement rather than an offer of employment.

An old case from 1964, *Edwards* v. *Skyways Ltd.*[6] provides that where an agreement has been reached in the course of business relations a heavy burden lies on the party suggesting that there was no intention to create legal relations. It is not enough, therefore, for the employer to assert that they had not intended to create a legal contract when providing an offer to a prospective employee. The *Edwards* case, in fact, concerned a payment of an *ex gratia* lump sum to redundant air crew and does not concern offers of employment but it is submitted that the same principle applies.

Another interesting example of how employers can get into difficulty **1.4** can be seen in *Gill* v. *Cape Contracts Ltd.*[7] The company sought to entice employees away from steady jobs with Harland and Woolf with promises of much higher paid jobs lasting for approximately six months at Sullom Voe in the Shetlands. The plaintiffs' employees were accepted for employment and were sent letters dated April 9, 1982, setting out terms and conditions of employment. They were to be paid £358 per week and so forth. They handed in their notice to Harland and Woolf who were upset and told them that they would not be employed by them again. On April 16, 1982, the company sent the plaintiffs telegrams telling them that they would not be able to employ them at Sullom Voe because union members in the Shetlands had objected to a labour force recruited in Northern Ireland. Accordingly they sued for breach of contract and the defendants resisted the claim by arguing that no binding contract had been made since they had not passed medicals which were a condition. All that had been offered was a reasonable

---

[5] [1979] I.R.L.R. 103.
[6] [1964] 1 All E.R. 494 and 1 W.L.R. 394.
[7] [1985] I.R.L.R. 499.

expectation that they would be employed. The Northern Irish Court rejected the argument that there was no contract upon which the plaintiffs were entitled to sue and held that the parties had entered into "collateral" contracts, consideration for which had been on the defendants part a promise of employment for approximately six months on agreed wage rates in return for the plaintiffs' agreement to give up their existing jobs. The representations as to wages and so forth constituted warranties to the collateral contracts, breaches of which entitled the plaintiffs to damages. The Court was clearly struck by the reality of the situation which was that the plaintiffs were, in the main, married men in steady employment and to give up that employment on a simple expectation would have been foolhardy in the extreme. It is slightly surprising that this case has not been more widely used but, perhaps, employers are not exposing themselves in this way.

Applications for Employment

1.5   Most employers will start with an advertisement, or alternatively some other form of invitation pursuant to which applicants will complete an application form. Small employers may say that it is not worth their while preparing some form of printed, or even typed, application form but it is suggested that it is false economy and that the application form itself can have advantages for the employer. The application form can ask questions in relation to previous criminal offences without contravening the terms of the Rehabilitation of Offenders Act 1974 (although the applicant need not necessarily answer in certain circumstances). This is not necessarily a sterile exercise. The application form contains details as to age, marital status, address, referees and the like and it may also contain details as to racial background and various other matters which are more controversial. In its most simple form the application will give the employer an opportunity to assess the handwriting and general standards of neatness and tidiness of the applicant. In contractual terms, it will create an "invitation" on behalf of the prospective employee.

Application Forms

1.6   There is set out in Appendix 2 a specimen application form. Apart from the basic information to which reference has been made above, *viz.* handwriting, name and address, *etc.,* key issues for application forms are age, educational qualifications and ethnic background. Sex and marital status also have relevance.

Selection of an Applicant

Care must be taken when selecting a candidate to avoid any possible discrimination.

Age Discrimination

In regard to age, it must be remembered that the imposition of an age **1.7** limit, whether upper or lower, can amount to the imposition of a condition with which fewer women can comply and thus to indirect discrimination against married women with young children under section 1(1)(*b*) of the Sex Discrimination Act 1975.[8] Price, a married woman aged 35 with two children was faced with an upper age limit of 28 which she thought was discriminatory of women because many in their twenties were involved in bringing up young children. The E.A.T. said that it should not be said a person could comply with a condition simply because it was theoretically possible. It was necessary to see whether they can in practice do so. Many women in their twenties are engaged in bearing and looking after children, and the case was remitted for a new hearing.

Geographic Discrimination

A requirement that an individual should or should not come from a **1.8** particular geographic area can constitute discrimination. There was a

---

[8] See *Price* v. *The Civil Service Commission* [1978] 1 All E.R. 1228, [1978] I.C.R. 27.

case involving Liverpool, which is divided into postal districts. It was shown that a higher proportion of coloured people live within certain postal districts in the centre of Liverpool than in others and, therefore, a restriction against applicants living in that postal area created a discrimination against coloured people. In *Hussein* v. *Saints Complete House Furnishers*[9] the employer's policy of not employing people living in the inner city area because of the tendency of their friends to hang around the shop was discriminatory of black people. 50 per cent of the population in that area was coloured as opposed to a coloured population of two per cent for Merseyside as a whole.

Education Discrimination

1.9   Educational qualifications can also give rise to potential discrimination. In *Meer* v. *London Borough of Tower Hamlets*[10] the Borough sought to impose educational qualifications with which fewer ethnic minority applicants could comply. Clearly the imposition of a requirement that educational qualifications should be solely related to the United Kingdom system creates a discrimination against anybody whose educational qualifications are not and could not have been attained through that system. Restrictions upon people's ability to speak languages or their appearance and dress are much less likely to create a discrimination, indeed most employers would say that the requirement that an applicant should speak English is not unreasonable. It might be, however, that employers would have to justify their reliance upon that requirement and show that it was justifiable within the meaning of the Act. As to justification see the case of *Ojutiku and Oburoni* v. *Manpower Services Commission.*[11] "Justifiable" involves a lower standard than necessary. It is justifiable if reasons for the requirement are given which would be acceptable to right-thinking people as sound and tolerable. The employer must prove the justification balancing the reasonable need against the discriminatory effect. This seems an eminently reasonable decision.

---

[9] [1979] I.R.L.R. 337.
[10] [1988] I.R.L.R. 399.
[11] [1982] I.R.L.R. 418.

Rehabilitation of Offenders Act 1974

Questions in relation to criminal offences can be asked in an **1.10**
application form. If the offence is "spent" under the Rehabilitation of
Offenders Act the applicant need not refer to it, but there is still some
point to such a question. For example, it is important to ask chauffeurs
or hauliers if they have ever been convicted of road traffic offences.

Ethnic Monitoring

Discrimination is not dealt with in this book as a separate topic: it **1.11**
warrants a book on its own. There are, however, some points mentioned
above, and here, which are highly relevant to recruitment and the
creation of the contract of employment. The insertion of a question as to
the applicant's racial origin in an application form is a highly conten-
tious matter. A number of employers consider it to be an unreasonable
infringement of the applicant's personal liberty. Others will say that it is a
perfectly reasonable question and without knowing the answer the
employer will have no idea whether or not their recruiters run the risk of
discriminating. To establish that fact it is necessary to have some
statistical material and, to have that, it is necessary to ask this question.
Indirect discrimination consists of applying a requirement or condition
which, whether intentional or not, adversely affects a considerably
larger portion of one racial group than others and cannot be justified on
non-racial grounds. A racial group is a group defined by reference to
colour, race, nationality (including citizenship or ethnic or national
origins). In their booklet *Monitoring an Equal Opportunity Policy*, the
Commission for Racial Equality say that the most effective form of
monitoring involves classifying all employees and job applicants
according to their ethnic origins and adding this information to personnel records, examining by ethnic origins the distribution of employees
and the success rate of applicants according to job, grade, department, *etc.,* and assessing the extent to which the distribution and
success rates reflect equal opportunity for all groups regardless of their
origins. They accept that the introduction of records along these lines
will be costly and time-consuming but assert that the usefulness of the

records outweighs those factors. They say that it is difficult to see how, without such records, an employer can find out exactly what is happening and can measure effectively the success of his equal opportunities policy. One further point not to be overlooked is that one added advantage of keeping records is that they may assist an employer to answer a complaint of racial discrimination at an industrial tribunal. This will, of course, be particularly so if the prospect of the burden of proof shifting firmly to an employer becomes a reality in the field of discrimination.

1.12 If individuals are asked to classify themselves, a specimen question could be as follows:

> "In order to help the company to ensure that its equal opportunity policy is being carried out, would you please provide the following information:
> I would describe my ethnic origin as. . . . "

1.13 Most recent (1989) guidance from C.R.E. suggests the following classifications:

> White
> Black—Caribbean
> Black—African
> Black—Other (please specify)
> Indian
> Pakistani
> Bangladeshi
> Chinese
> Other (please describe)

The C.R.E. emphasises that this is not the only classification that can be used and employers using other systems are not required to make any changes.

Contract Compliance

1.14 The Local Government Act 1988 generally requires scheduled public authorities to exercise their public supply and works contract functions without reference to non-commercial matters. Section 18(2) of the Act exempts local authorities from the requirement referred to above if they decide it is reasonably necessary to adopt a contract compliance scheme in order to fulfil their statutory duty under section 71 of the Race

Relations Act 1976. Section 71 says that, without prejudice to their obligation to comply with any other provision of the Act, it shall be the duty of every local authority to make appropriate arrangements with a view to establishing that their various functions are carried out with due regard to the need to eliminate unlawful racial discrimination and to promote equality of opportunity and good relations between persons of different racial groups.

The Commission for Racial Equality considers that the use of local **1.15** authority purchasing power provides them with an effective means of securing their objectives under that section and the C.R.E. is providing guidance to local authorities. This advice includes approved questions to be asked of suppliers to local authorities some of which deal with the question of whether or not it is the company's policy as an employer, to comply with its statutory obligations under the Race Relations Act. It also includes further detailed questions as to whether or not within the previous three years the company has had any finding of racial discrimination made against it, whether it has been the subject of any formal investigation, whether the company's policy is stated and, if so, where and so forth.

In what appears to be the first case on the point *R.* v. *The London* **1.16** *Borough of Islington ex parte The Building Employers Federation,*[12] Parker L.J. in the Divisional Court held, on an application for judicial review to determine whether the Islington Council's special contracts clauses requiring compliance with sections of the Sex Discrimination Act 1975 and health and safety legislation infringed the Local Government Act, that they did so. He said the purpose of the Act was to prevent local authorities from interfering with the provisions agreed between contractors and their workforces.

Notwithstanding, this should not deflect employers from giving very **1.17** serious consideration to providing in application forms a question designed to establish the ethnic origin of the applicant.

Job Offers

Offers have been dealt with above (see para. 1.3) and all that needs **1.18** to be added is to confirm that the employer should be careful to state precisely what it is that is being offered and if the offer constitutes a contract to be signed and returned, then the employer must take great

---

[12] Unreported—Divisional Court March 15, 1989.

care to refer where necessary to other documents and, in particular, to point out to the employee that reference documents may very well be changed. As has been said, the contract of employment is a dynamic thing, it grows, evolves and changes but the generally accepted view is that it cannot change beyond what was within the basic contemplation of the parties at the time the contract was created. Clearly the contract may change to the employee's detriment in minor ways but if any fundamental change is sought to be made which operates to the employee's detriment then difficulties will arise which will be dealt with in the section on variation below. Suffice it to say that a contract cannot be altered unilaterally to the substantial disadvantage of the employee without agreement. See Chapter 4 for authorities on variation.

Acceptance

1.19   The employer and the employee must be clear as to what it is they are accepting and the wording could be as follows:

> "I hereby acknowledge receipt of the statement of the terms and conditions of my employment of which this is a copy, together with copies of the following:
> 1.   The employee manual/rule book
> 2.   The guide to the pension fund rules
> 3.   . . .
> I accept the terms of these documents as being terms and conditions of my employment for the time being in force. I understand and accept that the terms of these documents may change from time to time and that I shall be bound by such changes."

1.20   There has been discussion about whether or not it is possible to consent in advance to an unknown change that is to be made to a contract. In *Breachin Bros.* v. *Kenneavy and Strand*[13] the written statements of terms and conditions stated that hours of work were as set out on notice boards and that any variation thereon would be similarly exhibited. On the facts, the employers never had a notice board and far less had any notices been exhibited thereon! Accordingly the tribunal doubted whether the provision had any meaning at all and the E.A.T.

---

[13] Unreported: E.A.T.: E.A.T. 373/82, 374/82.

agreed with that and also agreed with the conclusion that, in the circumstances, the contractual hours of work could only be measured by those which each employee had, in fact, worked. The employer must therefore ensure that there is an unequivocal right set out in the contract of employment and the simple fact that the statement of terms states that changes will be notified does not necessarily confer such a right.

In *Polymer Products Ltd.* v. *Prother*,[14] the employers knew that at some stage in the future they would have to move and they put a clause in the terms and conditions that employees "will be offered continuity of employment at any new location, with new duties, relocation allowance and salary all to be mutually agreed." When the company came to move they offered a driver a 10 per cent. increase in salary and one month's cost of living subsidy with certain changes in duties. He asked for more pay, it was refused and he resigned and claimed unfair constructive dismissal. The E.A.T. held that the clause in question was no more than an agreement to agree and was so uncertain as to be unenforceable. There was no obligation on the employer's part to make any offer to the employee and the making of the offer, albeit found to be inadequate, was not a breach of the contract giving rise to a constructive dismissal. Query whether it might have been a 'constructive redundancy' if the employers moved the whole business some distance and on a construction of the contract there was no 'mobility' obligation. In any event, note that a contract (an enforceable agreement) can only be made by an offer capable of acceptance on the one hand and acceptance of it on the other.

Start Date and Continuity

One matter in particular that must be dealt with clearly and precisely **1.21** is the date upon which the employment starts and any provision in relation to continuity from previous employment.

Parties to the Contract—Types of Status

The broad types to be considered are directors, agents, consultants, **1.22** independent contractors, loan out employees, seconded employees, agency arrangements, partners and casuals.

---

[14] Unreported: E.A.T. 599/80.

THE CONTRACT OF EMPLOYMENT

Directors

1.23   There is an overlap between the Companies Acts and the employment legislation in relation to directors. Directors are defined by section 741(1) of the 1985 Companies Act as "including any person occupying the position of director by whatever name called." This is entirely circular and there is no Companies Act definition of a director. A director can be an employee or not as the case may be and it is important that there is a clear understanding as to whether or not the director is an employee. A director is an office holder of the company and not necessarily its servant but if he enters into a service agreement or a contract of employment he will become a servant as well. Directors' contracts of employment are very often referred to as service agreements. A service agreement is simply a more sophisticated contract of employment. Very often there are some misconceptions about this. A director's service agreement may be express or implied and the courts will presume the existence of a contract of employment between the company and the director if the director is required to work full time for the company in return for a salary *Trussed Steel Concrete Co. Ltd.* v. *Green*[15] (although in that case the managing director might be an employee but was not employed at a particular address). As indicated, it is normal for directors to be provided with express service contracts or contracts of employment. The advantages are that such a document supercedes the E.P.C.A. section 1 statement and a copy can be made available for inspection by shareholders as required under section 318 of the Companies Act 1985. This section requires that every company shall have available for inspection by shareholders, in the case of each director whose contract is in writing, a copy of that contract and, in the case of each director whose contract is not in writing, a written memorandum setting out its terms. The contract will provide clear evidence of the employment relationship and all matters other than those contained simply in the written statement for section 1 purposes can be provided for in one document. The benefit to the director is that it provides him with security of employment because service contracts are usually contracts of employment for a fixed or indeterminate term and in the latter case terminable upon fairly lengthy notice, say, one year. A director can be removed from his office as a Companies Act director by a simple majority of votes at a general meeting of the company, whether or not there is any agreement to the contrary (section 303 of the Companies Act 1985). Nevertheless, if a director is removed

---

[15] [1946] 1 Ch. 114.

14

that will probably constitute a dismissal from his employment and he may have an action for breach of contract in addition to a claim for compensation for unfair dismissal. Very often directors' service contracts will provide that the employment should terminate if the directorship is terminated and vice versa. On the other side of the coin, the contract can also provide that a director cannot treat his being voted off the board as a constructive dismissal from his employment.

Certainty of the terms is generally to the benefit of both parties. **1.24** Success in enforcing oral contracts depends upon recollection, but carefully drafted contracts of employment will be of assistance. They can also include restrictive covenants, that is to say, restraints upon the employee's ability to work for competitors and the like after the termination of his employment.

It should be remembered that it is the duty of a director who is in any **1.25** way interested in a contract or proposed contract with the company to declare the nature of his interest and a director will, therefore, not be able to vote on his own contract. It should be remembered also that under the provisions of section 319 of the Companies Act 1985, if a director's service contract is for a period of more than five years the approval of the shareholders in general meeting is required, otherwise the company can terminate the contract at any time by giving reasonable notice. There are also Companies Act restrictions in the Companies Act on loans to directors, and prohibitions against dealing in share options. Directors are also covered by the provisions of the Company Securities (Insider Dealing) Act 1985. This provides that any individual who is, or at any time in the preceding six months has been, knowingly connected with the company shall not deal on a recognised stock exchange in securities of that company if he has information which he holds by virtue of being connected with the company and it would be reasonable to expect a person so connected not to disclose except in proper performance of his functions, and he knows it is unpublished price sensitive information. A person is connected with a company if he is a director of the company or occupies a position as an officer or employee.

Directors Service Contracts

A director's service contract or service agreement will contain **1.26** provisions not necessary or usual in a more "standard" contract of employment. At this stage it is worth noting some of the main points which should be dealt with. (See section 3.2 for more detail.)

THE CONTRACT OF EMPLOYMENT

Term, Job Title and Notice

1.27   In relation to term, it used to be fashionable to provide directors with five year service contracts, that fashion no longer prevails and three years is the maximum one would expect to see. The more familiar form would be for directors to have a one year rolling service contract. That is to say, a fixed term contract of one year is created but it does not expire by effluxion of time, it continues to roll on after the expiry of the first year until terminated by not less than one year's notice. The right to apply for compensation for unfair dismissal can be excluded if there is a contract for a fixed term of one year or more and the dismissal consists only of the expiry of the term without its being renewed if, before the term expires, the employee has agreed in writing to exclude any claim in respect of rights to apply for compensation for unfair dismissal. It would be quite normal, therefore, for a director's service contract to be for a fixed term for one year or more and for the director to agree to contract out of his right to claim for compensation for unfair dismissal if the service contract expires without being renewed. It is interesting to note that a contract can be for a fixed term, notwithstanding that there is a provision for notice during the term.

Directors Duties

1.28   This clause will provide broadly that the employee shall exercise and perform such powers and duties as the board may from time to time assign to him and that he will comply with all directions made by the board and be subject to the provisions of the relevant articles of association. It may provide for the employee to perform services not only for the company but also for other group companies and so forth. It may also provide for world-wide or United Kingdom-wide mobility:

> "If so directed and without any further remuneration, the executive shall perform his duties anywhere in the [United Kingdom] [world]."

Remuneration

1.29   This will provide for the annual salary and the manner of payment, any review perhaps by reference to the general index of retail prices (R.P.I.)

and any bonus provisions. If a bonus relates to net profit there will be a net profit clause. This means broadly the net consolidated profit arising from the trading of the company and any other group companies for the relevant financial year as shown by audited consolidated profit and loss accounts, whether prepared under historic cost convention or current cost accounting and subject to adjustments to ensure that the profit is taken before deducting tax and any commissions payable to the employee or other directors and so forth. The expenses provision may be in this clause or in a separate clause on its own which may also deal with car, credit cards, *etc.*

Pension and Insurance Schemes

1.30 This will involve a statement as to whether or not the employee is entitled to a pension and whether or not a contracting out certificate is in force, whether the company operates a contributory scheme or non-contributory scheme and whether or not the employee is eligible or obliged to join. Accident and disability insurance policies will be dealt with, as will medical insurance policies including permanent health schemes.

Holidays

1.31 This will, very often, speak for itself and be a simple clause.

Illness

1.32 It is quite usual to provide that if a senior executive is incapable of performing his duties for a period of, say, three months in any period of 12 consecutive months then the company may terminate the employment. The clause will deal with the question of payment during periods of incapacity and the interrelation between these provisions and any insurance scheme provisions. (See also Chapter 8 below.)

THE CONTRACT OF EMPLOYMENT

Termination

1.33 It sometimes comes as a surprise to employers to know that it is not possible to terminate a fixed term contract during the term for incompetence unless there is either a termination provision, or the incompetence is of such an order that it can be said the employee has been in fundamental breach of his obligations under the contract. A termination clause will be without prejudice to the fixed term and will provide that the employment can be terminated if the employee commits a material or persistent breach of the contract, mis-manages the business of the company or any group company, is guilty of any conduct tending to bring himself or the company into disrepute and if the employee becomes of unsound mind or commits an act of bankruptcy or compounds with his creditors generally. There may also be a provision for suspension on full pay and provisions dealing with what happens upon termination including a provision that the employee will resign as a director and so forth.

Limitation provisions—restrictive covenants

1.34 There will normally be limitation provisions which will deal with non competition during the employment and after the termination of the employment, confidentiality of trade secrets, solicitation of employees and customers after the termination of the employment and generally. These are extremely sensitive and complex matters and they need very considerable care and attention. The law generally leans against covenants in restraint of trade and if the employer wishes to restrain the employee from carrying on certain activities after the termination of employment, which might otherwise operate to the commercial disadvantage of the employer, then very careful drafting of the limitation clauses will be required.

Appointment of Agent and Waiver of Rights

1.35 There may well be a clause pursuant to which the employee irrevocably appoints somebody to be his agent to execute documents so that if he is away or becomes incapacitated, professional life can go on. The employee may well be asked to waive rights against the company in the event that the employment is terminated prematurely by reason of any scheme of amalgamation or reconstruction provided the employee is offered employment in the amalgamated or reconstructed entity. This clause will also deal with the contracting out of the employee's rights to a redundancy payment and compensation for unfair dismissal by virtue of the expiry of the term of the employment without it being renewed.

The Golden Parachute

In order to recruit and/or retain key people, some employers provide **1.36** "golden parachutes" which provide for payment of a sum as liquidated damages if following a takeover the employee gives notice within a specified period, or the takeover itself gives the employee the right to treat the contract as repudiated. Subject to such clauses being within the scope of the Memorandum and Articles of the company and in the interest of the company, such clauses are acceptable but need very careful drafting.

Grievance Procedure

It is sometimes thought it is not appropriate to involve senior execu- **1.37** tives in grievance and disciplinary procedures but a short grievance procedure clause is sometimes of some value.

Miscellaneous

There will then be some miscellaneous provisions in relation to, for **1.38** example, the service of notice, definitions, addresses for service, the fact that the contract constitutes the entire contract between the parties and is in substitution for any previous arrangement and possibly the fact that the agreement is governed by and construed in accordance with the laws of England.

THE CONTRACT OF EMPLOYMENT

Agents, Consultants and Independent Contractors

1.39 As has been indicated above, attention should be paid to whether or not a contract is for service, that is to say employment, or the provision of services which will not be an employment. Consultants and independent contractors will usually provide services to the company and the company will be very careful to ensure that they are not treated as employees. The four main indicia of a contract of employment are the employer's power of selecting his employee, the payment of wages or other remuneration, the employer's right to control the method of doing the work and the employer's right of suspension or dismissal.[16] The right of control can very often be decisive and the test is right rather than actual control. The independent contractor undertakes to produce a given result but is free to use his own discretion as to how he does it, except perhaps in matters specified beforehand. Lord Denning has said:

> "Under a contract of service, a man is employed as part of the business and his work is done as an integral part of the business; whereas under a contract for services his work, though done for the business, is not integrated into it."

An agent is merely a person with authority to do some act on behalf of another and to represent him. A bailee is entrusted with possession or goods for a particular purpose. He is his own master and has possession of goods bailed to him whereas a servant has custody only. A policeman's powers derive from his office rather than from the local authority employing him and the local authority is, accordingly, not vicariously liable for his acts.[17] A director used perhaps to be considered to be the agent of the company rather than the servant of the company. The director is now almost always an employee. Partners are not the employees of the firm but each partner is the agent of the other partners in respect of partnership matters. A contract for the employment of an employee employed by a partnership does not itself make the employee a partner in the business (Partnership Act 1890, s.2).

1.40 These are relatively old-fashioned precepts but important in distinguishing between contracts of employment and contracts for the

---

[16] See *Short* v. *J.W. Henderson Ltd.* [1946] 62 T.L.R. 427.
[17] See *Fisher* v. *Oldham Corp.* [1930] 2 K.B. 364.

provision of services. It will very often be important for the employer to incur no tax liability in respect of independent contractors and to prevent such people from having or achieving employment protection rights, be they in relation to compensation, redundancy, maternity or for whatever. The use of an independent agency will achieve this result provided the agency is genuine, independent and conducts its affairs properly.

Employees as Independant Contractors

The most significant case in relation to deciding whether or not **1.41** individuals are employees is *O'Kelly* v. *Trust House Forte plc*.[18] In that case, the Court of Appeal held that the question of whether a contract is one of service or for services is a pure question of law as is also the test that has to be applied to the facts in order to reach a decision in any particular case. It is for the tribunal of fact not only to find the facts but also to assess them qualitatively and that assessment dictates the correct legal answer. An appellate court can only interfere with a tribunal's decision on the point if the tribunal have misdirected themselves in law or reached a decision which no tribunal properly directed on the facts could have reached.

Section 153(1) of E.P.C.A. states that an employee is an individual **1.42** who has entered into or works under (or, where the employment has ceased, worked under) a contract of employment.

> " 'Contract of employment' means a contract of service or apprenticeship, whether express or implied, and (if it is express) whether it is oral or in writing."

O'Kelly and two others were waiters engaged on a casual basis by **1.43** the respondents in their banquetting department. They complained of unfair dismissal and the tribunal considered as a preliminary point whether or not they were employees. They concluded that they were not, rather that they were independent contractors engaged on separate contracts for services each time they reported for work as waiters. On appeal the EAT dealt with the question of jurisdiction which depended upon whether the question was one of fact or law and held on the authority of the Court of Appeal's decision in *Young and Woods Ltd.* v. *West*[19] that it was a question of law on which there was a right and a wrong answer and on which they could make up their minds on

---

[18] [1983] I.R.L.R. 369.
[19] [1980] I.R.L.R. 202.

the facts found by the tribunal. The employers appealed successfully to the Court of Appeal on that particular point. Lord Justice Donaldson said it is only if the weight given to a particular factor shows a self misdirection in law that an appellate court with a limited jurisdiction can interfere. Quite apart from these nice points on the relative jurisdictions of the industrial tribunals and the Employment Appeal Tribunal, the case is of considerable value in setting out those factors which are consistent or inconsistent with individuals being employees:

1.44 Factors Consistent with Employment:

1. The applicants provided their services in return for remuneration for work actually performed. They did not invest their own capital or stand to gain or lose from the commercial success of the functions organised by the banqueting department.
2. They performed their work under the direction and control of the respondents.
3. When the casual workers attended a function they were part of the respondents organisation and for the purposes of ensuring the smooth running of the business they were represented in the staff consultation process.
4. When working they were carrying on the business of the respondents.
5. Clothing and equipment were provided by the respondents.
6. The applicants were paid weekly in arrears and were paid under deduction of Income Tax and Social Security contributions.
7. Their work was organised on the basis of a weekly rota and they required permission to take time off from rostered duties.
8. There was a disciplinary and grievance procedure.
9. There was holiday pay and incentive bonus calculated by reference to past service.

1.45 Factors Inconsistent with Employment:

1. The engagement was terminable without notice on either side.
2. The applicants had the right to decide whether or not to accept work; whether or not it would be in their interest to exercise the right to refuse work was another matter.
3. The respondents had no obligation to provide any work.

4. During the subsistence of the relationship it was the parties view that casual workers were independent contractors engaged under successive contracts for services.
5. It is recognised custom and practice of the industry that casual workers are engaged under a contract for services.
6. The most important ingredient was mutuality of obligation.

In another case, *Wickens* v. *Champion Employment*[20] The E.A.T. held that:

"although there was not evidence that the temporaries were carrying on business on their own account, they were under no obligation to accept bookings offered by the employers and the employers had no obligation to find work for them; that the contracts between the employers and the temporaries did not create a relationship that had the elements of continuity and care associated with the relationship created by a contract of employment; that, accordingly, the industrial tribunal had not erred in law in determining that the temporaries were not employees and, therefore, they had no jurisdiction to hear the applicant's complaint of unfair dismissal."

In *Norwich Pty. Ltd.* v. *Commissioner of Pay-Roll Tax*[21] the Privy Counsel *per* Lord Brandon held that:

"the principles of law were well settled relating to the determination of the question whether, in any particular case, a person who did work for another and received remuneration in respect of such work was an employee or an independent contractor. The principles stated by the Judicial Committee in *Australian Mutual Provident Society* v. *Chaplin and Another*[22] were applicable to a case of the present kind.
The effect of the contract as a whole was to create between the company and the lecturer the relationship of employer and employee, and the clause which purported to provide otherwise failed in its purpose. A lecturer was tied hand and foot by the contract with regard to the manner of performing the work under it, and in those circumstances the only possible conclusion was that the lecturer was an employee."

In *Young & Woods Ltd.* v. *West*[23] Mr West wished to be taxed under **1.46** Schedule D (for self employed people) and had Revenue agreement for this. Subsequently he wished to say he was employed and to claim compensation for unfair dismissal. To do this he had to assert that he was an employee. He did so assert before the Court of Appeal and they

---

[20] [1984] I.C.R. 365.
[21] [1984] I.C.R. 286.
[22] [1978] 18 All E.R. 385.
[23] [1980] I.R.L.R. 201.

agreed with him. They looked at the reality not just the words of the contract. In the judgments some harsh things were said about him and the Court of Appeal thought the Inland Revenue would have to reopen his old assessments!

1.47 The wise employer will, however discuss these matters with the Revenue and, indeed, there is encouragement for this in paragraph 2 of the Revenue booklet *Employers' Guide to P.A.Y.E.* It must be remembered that under the P.A.Y.E. regulations the burden of making all proper P.A.Y.E. deductions falls on the employer and although, in the event that incorrect deductions are made, the employer may have a right to go against the employee at a later stage, by that time it may be too late and the employees may have dispersed or alternatively not have the funds. It should be remembered also that employees who work for less than 16 hours a week do not obtain employment protection; however, they are employees. It should also be remembered that the definition of employment under the Equal Pay Act 1970 and Sex Discrimination Act 1975 is wider than that under E.P.C.A.

> "Employment under a contract of service or of apprenticeship or a contract personally to execute any work or labour."

1.48 In *Quinnen* v. *Howells*[24] the E.A.T. held that this phrase was intended to enlarge upon the ordinary connotation of employment so as to include persons outside the employer/employee relationship:

> "The present case confirms that those who engage, even cursorily, the talents, skills or labour of the self employed are wise to ensure that the terms are equal as between men and women and do not discriminate between them."

1.49 The definition in the Race Relations Act 1976 is also the wide definition. There has been recent authority in connection with sex discrimination and the Mirror Group Newspapers and its agents. *Mirror Group Newspapers Ltd.* v. *Gunning.*[25] The words "a contract personally to execute any work or labour" in the Sex Discrimination Act contemplate a contract whose dominant purpose is that the party contracting to provide services under it performs personally the work or labour which forms the subject-matter of the contract. The dominant purpose here was distribution of newspapers so there could be no jurisdiction to entertain a complaint of sex discrimination.

---

[24] [1988] I.R.L.R. 227.
[25] [1986] I.R.L.R. 27.

Secondments, Transfers, etc.

This is an area where, again, great care needs to be taken in **1.50** deciding quite what the employer is trying to achieve. If employees are seconded, then attention needs to be paid as to who remains the employer and who has control over the employees in question. It is quite possible to structure the arrangements so that the original employer remains the employer, albeit that the control and direction of the employees work is governed by the company to whom the employee is seconded. The employee will remain paid by the base company and all documentation will be processed through that company, albeit that there may be a recovery by way of a service charge levied on the company to whom the employee is seconded.

These arrangements are particularly significant if groups of com- **1.51** panies have a service company that is the employing company for the group. In those circumstances, it seems that it is desirable to have inter company agreements that regulate the provision of employees to the group trading companies and the inter company payments that arise. VAT issues will need to be considered and whether or not the group service company charges more than 100 per cent. of the employment costs to the trading companies. Such inter company agreements can regulate the questions of control and discipline referred to above in whichever manner is considered most effective for that particular group.

Partners

Partners are not employees unless they are salaried partners in which **1.52** event they will be employees working under that particular title and no special considerations will attach to them save that they have the capacity to bind their fellow non-salaried partners contractually since they are held out to the world as being partners in the business.

Casuals

In a sense, casuals are covered by all the remarks made above in **1.53** relation to consultants and independent contractors. If casuals are not employees, it must be made quite plain that there is no mutuality of obligation between the parties. That is one of the acid tests for deciding whether or not an individual is an employee or whether the relationship of employer and employee subsists. If the employer cannot require the individual to attend for work and if the individual cannot require the employee to provide work, then no employment relationship will subsist. Some employers have banks of individuals upon whom they rely when there are heavy workloads and they would rather use individuals who have, perhaps, in the past been employees to deal with these peaks of work rather than temporaries or other types of staff. Employers should take great care to ensure that, if they do not wish to, they do not create an employment relationship. Documentation should make the position in relation to holidays and sick pay, etc., entirely clear and the documentation should avoid so far as is possible comparable references to employees. For example, in relation to disciplinary procedures, it is probably not appropriate to have them for casual workers. No doubt, for the sake of good industrial relations, companies would wish to discuss these matters with "on call" individuals and, perhaps, there ought to be separate procedures but it would be dangerous to invoke the same disciplinary procedure as is available for employees. An example of the sort of wording that might be used in communications to such individuals is as follows:

> "It is confirmed that the arrangements pursuant to which you provide services to the company are ad hoc. When you are offered work the company will try to give you as much notice as possible but it must be clear from the outset there is no obligation either on the company to offer you work or on you to accept any work that may be offered. You are not an employee of the company.
> You are not entitled to any fringe benefits including, for example, sick pay, holidays or pension rights.
> You will be paid only for the hours actually worked at the rate of £[   ] per day and it has been agreed with the Revenue that there will be deductions of tax as if you are an employee but this is for administrative purposes only."

1.54 This highlights a particular concern in relation to P.A.Y.E. Entering into a specific arrangement with the Revenue in these circumstances is of enormous benefit to the employer. Absent this, the employer is likely not to deduct P.A.Y.E and rely upon the individuals in question to satisfy all Revenue requirements. This is not always something that the employer can guarantee will happen.

Status of Statutory Written Particulars of Contract— Section 1 E.P.C.A. 1978

If a contract of employment has been created and whether it be oral **1.55** or in writing there is a statutory obligation on the employer under section 1 of the Employment Protection (Consolidation) Act 1978 (referred to throughout the book as "E.P.C.A.") to provide within 13 weeks after the beginning of an employee's period of employment with an employer, a written statement in accordance with the provisions of the section. The written particulars are set out in Appendix 1 and include obligations to state the parties, the date when the employment began, whether any employment with the previous employer counts as part of the employee's continuous period of employment, the amount and rate of pay, terms as to hours of work and normal working hours, holidays and holiday pay, any terms relating to sick pay, any provisions relating to pensions, length of notice, job title and any disciplinary or grievance rules or grievance procedures. There is also an obligation to state whether or not a contracting out certificate is in force for the particular employment. A contracting out certificate is a certificate stating whether or not the employment is contracted out of the State pension scheme. If a certificate is not provided, then the employer and employee will pay the relevant National Insurance contributions to the State and the employee will ultimately be in receipt of a state pension.

In Writing

If, therefore, a contract is oral there is an overwhelming argument for **1.56** reducing its terms to writing because of the obligation to notify the employee in writing of these matters. Where an employer does not give an employee a statement required under section 1 of E.P.C.A. the employee may refer the matter to an industrial tribunal to enforce compliance with the section. The tribunal has fairly wide ranging powers including the power to confirm the particulars given already, amend those particulars or, even, substitute other particulars for them as may be appropriate.

THE CONTRACT OF EMPLOYMENT

Pay Statement

1.57   Section 8 of E.P.C.A. provides that every employee shall have the right to be given by his employer, at or before the time at which any payment of wages or salary is made, an itemised pay statement in writing containing particulars as to the gross amount of wages or salary, the amounts of any variable or fixed deductions from that gross amount and the purposes for which they have been made, the net amount of wages or salary and where different parts of the net amount are paid in different ways, the amount and method of payment of each part payment. If a Tribunal finds that an employer has failed to give an employee a pay statement in accordance with section 8 of E.P.C.A., then the tribunal may make a declaration to that effect and further may make an order that the employer pay the employee any sums which may have been made by way of unnotified deductions from pay.

Other Statutory Requirements

1.58   There are some other subsidiary matters in relation to section 1 of E.P.C.A. which are of some significance. If a contract is for a fixed term then the statement of particulars must state the date when the contract expires. A statement under section 1 may, for all or any of the particulars to be given by the statement, refer the employee to some document which the employee has reasonable opportunities of reading in the course of his employment, or which is made reasonably access-ible to him. It is not necessary to provide a statement for any employ-ment when the hours of employment are normally less than 16 hours per week. If, after the statement has been given there is a change in the terms of employment, the employer must not more than one month after the change inform the employee of the nature of the change by a written statement, but again this can be done by reference to some document which the employee has reasonable opportunities of reading, or which is made reasonably accessible to him. If the name of the employer is changed without any change in the corporate identity of the employer, that is to say it is a simple company name change, or the actual identity of the employer is changed so that, for example, an associated company becomes the employer for internal reorganisation purposes so that continuity of employment is not broken and there is no other change in terms, a fresh statement of terms is not required, simply a statement notifying the employee of the nature of the change.

The obligation to provide this written statement does not apply to an **1.59** employee if the contract of employment is one which has been reduced to writing in one or more documents and which contains express terms satisfying the provisions of section 1, provided that the employee has been given a copy of the contract and he has been provided with a statement of disciplinary and grievance procedures or has had a reasonable opportunity of reading those procedures or they are accessible to him in a convenient form.

Cleary, this means that this adds further weight to the argument that **1.60** contracts should be put in writing and provided to employees. The provision of a contract satisfies the requirement to provide written particulars, provided of course all the matters set out in section 1 are contained in the contract.

Please note, however, that the converse does not apply. There is **1.61** authority that the contract is not necessarily exclusively set out in a written statement of particulars under section 1 of E.P.C.A. In *Turriff Construction Ltd.* v. *Bryant & Others*[26] in the Divisional Court it was held that a statutory statement of terms is not an employment contract and, indeed, that it is not even conclusive evidence of the contract's terms. Bryant and others started work and were given a statutory statement of terms under the then provisions of section 4 of the Contracts of Employment Act 1963 which referred to a working rule agreement providing for a basic 40 hour week. Later a site agreement between employer and union purported to vary the hours to 51 and notices were put up from time to time. Not one of the respondents was ever forced to, or ever did, work 51 hours and when they were made redundant it was held on appeal that the payments should be calculated on the basis of the 40 hour week. It was held that the site agreement could not be construed as a variation of the respondents' contracts so as to compel them to work 51 hours a week and it was quite clear that the statutory statement was not a contract itself.

This decision was upheld by the E.A.T. in 1981 in *System Floors* **1.62** *(U.K.) Ltd.* v. *Daniel*[27] Daniel started work in 1979 as an agency worker. In November he started work as an employee of the company. Three months thereafter he was given a statutory statement of terms under section 1 of E.P.C.A. which showed that he started employment on November 19. He signed this to acknowledge receipt and was dismissed on November 14 the following year. When he applied for unfair dismissal compensation there was a dispute as to whether or not he had sufficient length of service so that the tribunal had jurisdiction. The then

---

[26] [1967] 2 K.I.R. 659.
[27] [1981] I.R.L.R. 475.

THE CONTRACT OF EMPLOYMENT

The obligation to provide this written statement does not apply to an **1.59** employee if the contract of employment is one which has been reduced to writing in one or more documents and which contains express terms satisfying the provisions of section 1, provided that the employee has been given a copy of the contract and he has been provided with a statement of disciplinary and grievance procedures or has had a reasonable opportunity of reading those procedures or they are accessible to him in a convenient form.

Cleary, this means that this adds further weight to the argument that **1.60** contracts should be put in writing and provided to employees. The provision of a contract satisfies the requirement to provide written particulars, provided of course all the matters set out in section 1 are contained in the contract.

Please note, however, that the converse does not apply. There is **1.61** authority that the contract is not necessarily exclusively set out in a written statement of particulars under section 1 of E.P.C.A. In *Turriff Construction Ltd.* v. *Bryant & Others*[26] in the Divisional Court it was held that a statutory statement of terms is not an employment contract and, indeed, that it is not even conclusive evidence of the contract's terms. Bryant and others started work and were given a statutory statement of terms under the then provisions of section 4 of the Contracts of Employment Act 1963 which referred to a working rule agreement providing for a basic 40 hour week. Later a site agreement between employer and union purported to vary the hours to 51 and notices were put up from time to time. Not one of the respondents was ever forced to, or ever did, work 51 hours and when they were made redundant it was held on appeal that the payments should be calculated on the basis of the 40 hour week. It was held that the site agreement could not be construed as a variation of the respondents' contracts so as to compel them to work 51 hours a week and it was quite clear that the statutory statement was not a contract itself.

This decision was upheld by the E.A.T. in 1981 in *System Floors* **1.62** *(U.K.) Ltd.* v. *Daniel*[27] Daniel started work in 1979 as an agency worker. In November he started work as an employee of the company. Three months thereafter he was given a statutory statement of terms under section 1 of E.P.C.A. which showed that he started employment on November 19. He signed this to acknowledge receipt and was dismissed on November 14 the following year. When he applied for unfair dismissal compensation there was a dispute as to whether or not he had sufficient length of service so that the tribunal had jurisdiction. The then

---

[26] [1967] 2 K.I.R. 659.
[27] [1981] I.R.L.R. 475.

and conditions of employment which prevail in the work place and an agreement that the employee is bound by those terms. It is a fine distinction but it is suggested that employers would be wise to cover themselves by ensuring that the employee agrees that the terms and conditions are an accurate statement of the terms and conditions prevailing and, indeed, that the employee is bound thereby.

Status of Section 1 Particulars

The status of written statements under section 1 of E.P.C.A. was **1.64** considered again in *Robertson* v. *British Gas Corp.*[29] by the Court of Appeal in 1982. In that case the Court of Appeal relied on *Turriff Construction Ltd.* v. *Bryant & Others* (see paragraph 1.61), which was followed in *System Floors (U.K.) Ltd.* v. *Daniel*. The Court of Appeal held that the terms of the contract of employment were to be found in the letter of appointment which had been provided to employees, that the terms of a collective agreement in relation to a bonus scheme were expressly imported into the contract of employment and that a purported unilateral determination of that collective agreement could not affect the tariff under the scheme. This case is also interesting and helpful in relation to the vexed question as to the status of collective agreements in relation to individual contracts of employment. There is further discussion of this below. The key point for these purposes however, is that the Court of Appeal held that if there is a conflict between the letter of appointment which they had already decided constituted the terms of the contract and the statutory statement which had also been provided to the employees in question, then the letter of appointment took precedence.

Interestingly, in *Jones* v. *Associated Tunnelling Co. Ltd.*[30] in the E.A.T. **1.65** in 1981, Mr. Justice Browne-Wilkinson held that a statutory statement on its own cannot effect a contractual variation but where the employee is silent and continues to work under varied terms without objecting, this might amount to an implied agreement to the variation. He did point out that the view should be adopted only cautiously and mainly in respect of terms with immediate practical effect, like, for example, pay rates. That case was, in fact, a mobility case and will be dealt with later in relation not only to variation but also mobility.

---

[29] [1983] I.R.L.R. 302.
[30] [1981] I.R.L.R. 477, E.A.T.

1.66 An interesting example of how the employee's remedy works in cases where a statutory statement has not been provided can be found in the decision of the Court of Appeal in the case of *Mears* v. *Safecar Security*.[31]

---

[31] [1982] 3 W.L.R. 366.

CHAPTER 2

STRUCTURE OF THE CONTRACT

Content

2.1 It is submitted that a simple form with relevant headings and space for relevant details to be completed, whilst being perfectly adequate to comply with section 1 of E.P.C.A. does not go far enough either for employer or for employee and the proper course is for employers to provide a proper contract of employment to employees. Reference can perfectly properly be made in such contract to other documents and, indeed, very often is. However, this should not stop the employer providing a contract which can be kept up to date from time to time as the law develops.

2.2 The contract should be headed with the name of the employer and provide a section for the name of the employee. It should then specify the precise starting date and whether or not there has been any previous service which counts for continuity purposes.

2.3 The contract is easier to read if it is divided into numbered sections each of which has a heading. A suggested schedule of headings is set out below:

(1)   Job Title, Grade or Category.

(2)   Place of Work and any Mobility Obligation.

STRUCTURE OF THE CONTRACT

(3)   Any Provision as to Probationary Period.

(4)   Salary/Pay

Specifying the annual or weekly amount, when it is paid and whether it is paid in advance or in arrears or half and half. Whether this section should be the appropriate place to deal with any allowances is a matter of style. Quite often allowances, bonuses and the like will be dealt with by reference in another document.

(5)   Hours of Work

2.4   Specifying both normal hours of work, the length of the normal working week, whether a lunch break is allowed and, if so, of how long and whether it is paid or unpaid. If the employee is working on shift then this is the appropriate place to so specify. It is also the appropriate place to specify overtime obligations if appropriate, the amount of time that has to be completed before overtime qualifies the employee for any extra payment and the rates of extra payment. Whether overtime working on weekends and bank holidays needs to be dealt with in this section is, again, a matter of style. Those matters should not, however, be overlooked. In particular the contract should specify whether time off in lieu can be taken and, if so, whether it has to be taken by agreement or on what terms.

(6)   Holidays

2.5   Holidays will almost always be paid holidays. However, if there is any provision for taking time off for certain activities on an unpaid basis (or indeed even on a paid basis), this will probably be the appropriate place to specify unless there is a separate section dealing with time off work for trade union activities, for example. In sections dealing with holidays it is necessary to deal with the holiday year, whether it be the calendar year or otherwise, whether holiday has to be taken within the holiday year, whether prior permission has to be obtained before any holiday can be agreed and whether any payment in lieu of holiday entitlements can be made. Clearly entitlements have to be specified and appropriate pro-rating arrangements made for those who join during a holiday year.

(7) Sickness and Sick Pay Provisions

It is very important to specify in a contractual document that **2.6** employees have an obligation to notify the employer as soon as possible on any day on which the employee is unable to attend work by reason of ill health (or, indeed, any other absence). Some sickness or sick pay clauses will refer generally to absences, whether by reason of ill health or otherwise. Now that the employer has control of the Statutory Sick Pay scheme, it is very important that contractual obligations are imposed upon employees to deal with absences by reason of sickness in a proper manner. Most employers will provide for some level of pay during absences by reason of sickness in excess of the Statutory Sick Pay requirements and that provision of pay will have to be dealt with in the contract. For example, if an employee has been employed for, say, five years, then it may be appropriate to pay the employee during periods of certified absence by reason of sickness for a period of, say, two months during any 12 calendar months and that any further absences, by reason of sickness, will only be paid at the rate of 50 per cent. or whatever. There will need to be provisions for meshing the Statutory Sick Pay provisions into any occupational or contractual sick pay scheme so that occupational sick pay (O.S.P.) will be reduced by the amount of Statutory Sick Pay (S.S.P.). It will be necessary to specify what happens to bonuses and allowances during any period of absence by reason of sickness. There is, in some industries, a tendency for employees to consider that they can take, as it were as extra holiday, any amount of sickness absence in respect of which the employer provides full pay. Employers should strive to avoid any references to the use of the word "leave" or other wording that suggests some sort of permissiveness in relation to absence by reason of sickness and to regulate fairly strictly, if necessary, any periods during which employees are in receipt of full pay whilst absent by reason of sickness. Sickness should be an exception, not a rule and, indeed, employers may well wish to look very carefully at their record keeping systems in relation to absences generally so that, if employees are regularly sick on Fridays or Mondays, appropriate steps can be taken to consider that with the employee and, if appropriate, turn the matter from one of concession to one of discipline. (Please refer also to Chapter 8 below for a detailed discussion of Statutory Sick Pay and Occupational Sick Pay).

(8) Medical Reports

2.7 Access to Medical Reports Act 1988. Please see Appendix 3 for a specimen form for reference to a company doctor.

(9) Notice to Terminate the Contract

2.8 There must be provisions in relation to the notice to be given by employer and by employee. If the employer relies upon the statutory minimum periods of notice then those should be set out and there should be specification as to whether or not the notice must be given in writing and to whom and so on.

(10) Retirement age

2.9 It is worth considering having a separate section in relation to retirement age as opposed to the pension section. The whole issue of retirement is in a state of flux at the moment whilst the Government tries to make up its mind what to do with the State retirement age, although there is a provision in the Employment Bill 1989 to equalise the redundancy age at 60. The concept of a contractual retirement age is a difficult one because it is, in reality, a contractual provision which sets out the date or age at which the employer can require the employee to leave employment by way of retirement. Technically, this creates a dismissal, albeit almost certainly a fair dismissal, provided that no unfairness operates in the way that the retirement age is enforced and provided also that there is no discrimination between men and women. It is also important to distinguish in the employers mind between a date under the contract at which employees can be required to retire, that is to say a contractual retirement age and a normal retirement age which can, in some circumstances, be different. If a substantial majority of employees of a particular category or kind or level all retire at a particular age which by custom and practice is different from the age provided for in any contractual documentation, then there is an over-whelming argument for saying that the normal retirement age for those within that particular category is the age at which they would normally retire rather than the age provided for in the contract. The contract should, however, provide for the age at which the employer expects or requires the employee to retire.

(11) Pensions

Whether the employer operates a contributory or non contributory **2.10** scheme should be specified as, indeed, should the issue as to whether or not the employment is contracted out under the provisions of the Social Security Pensions Act 1975. The date of joining any scheme, eligibility and so forth should be specified in brief and reference made to appropriate pension fund rules. Please refer to Chapter 10 for a more detailed analysis of the interrelation between the contract and the pension.

(12) Grievance Procedure and Disciplinary Procedures

There should be provision for grievance and disciplinary procedures **2.11** however short and simple they may be. It would, in certain circum-stances, be appropriate to have a grievance procedure which provided simply that the employee should raise any grievance with his or her immediate superior who will deal with the matter appropriately. Very often, however, grievance procedures and disciplinary procedures will be dealt with by reference to another document which sets them out in detail. Great care should be taken to ensure that grievance and disciplinary procedures are simple and readily understandable and comply so far as is possible with the A.C.A.S. code of practice.

(13) Trade Unions

Whether the employer wishes to make any statement in relation to **2.12** trade unions, the recognition thereof and the right to join them will vary depending upon the industry and the inclination of the employer.

(14)   Health and Safety at Work

2.13   Some employers will wish to provide in contractual documentation a health and safety at work policy statement, others will consider it inappropriate and deal with their obligations under that legislation by reference.

(15)   Equal Opportunities and Race and Sex Discrimination

2.14   Again some employers will wish to state their equal opportunity policy in brief in contractual documentation and some will wish to refer to it by reference and others will wish not to refer to it by reference or in the contract but simply have stated elsewhere their policy in this regard.

(16)   General Terms

2.15   As has been emphasized before, there should be a clear statement of what documents are incorporated by reference, the fact that such documents have been provided to the employee (or an indication where they can be read) and a clear and unequivocal statement that the employer reserves the right to change terms and conditions of employment from time to time and that such changes will be binding upon the employee. The employee should acknowledge receipt of the documents and confirm that the employee is bound by the terms and conditions of employment provided to him and communicated to him from time to time.

Sources of Terms and Conditions

2.16   Generally, the sources of terms and conditions are the contract of employment, the statutory statement of terms and conditions, the rule book, any handbook, collective agreements and pension fund documentation. The first matter that falls for consideration is whether the employer wants to incorporate the terms of these documents into the contract. It is very important that employers should consider carefully whether or not particular matters are ones of contract or are considered to be "non-contractual."

When considering whether a matter is one of discretion or of contract, **2.17** alternatively whether notwithstanding something has been considered to be a matter of concession, an employee could nonetheless sue for it or on it, it has always seemed to the author that there is a real risk to an employer if discretion is continually exercised over a period of time. If, for example, a bonus scheme is expressed to be discretionary but nonetheless the employer makes payments under the scheme every year for, say, 10 years, it seems that notwithstanding the fact that it purports to be a discretionary bonus scheme the employee could nonetheless say that it had taken on the guise of something beyond discretion and a matter of obligation. In *Frishers Ltd.* v. *Taylor*,[1] Mr. Justice Talbot held that where a full weeks wage was paid to every employee as a Christmas bonus for several years, this constituted an implied term of their employment contracts. It was a breach of this term when an employee was paid only half a week's wages due to an alleged unsatisfactory performance. In this case the employee resigned and claimed compensation for unfair constructive dismissal. All other employees had been given a full week's wages as a bonus and she had been given only half a week's wages. The evidence established that for several years previously all employees including her had been given Christmas bonuses based on a weeks wages. The employers resisted her claim on the grounds that the bonus was discretionary and that the reason she was given a small bonus was because of her poor performance. The view that the size of the bonus depended upon satisfactory performance had never been communicated to the employees and the industrial tribunal found that she had been con-structively dismissed because the receipt of a bonus of a week's wages had become implied into her and other employees contracts. The employer's appeal to the E.A.T. was unsuccessful. The E.A.T. said that there was evidence that the bonus had been regularly paid to the respondent and to others over the years—it had become part of the remuneration that she and the other employees were entitled to expect to receive. There had never been any suggestion so far as could be seen from the findings of fact that it was purely a matter of discretion until this change of policy. In the view of the E.A.T. there was evidence to found an implied term—there had been consistent conduct throughout the years and it was right to regard that as a term of the contract which had to be implied in law into the contract in relation

---

[1] Unreported E.A.T. 336/729.

to the payment of remuneration. How long a bonus has to be paid before it becomes a part of the contract is a moot point but clearly employers would do well to consider right at the outset whether matters are matters of discretion and whether they are matters of contract. Certain items are sometimes divided into contractual benefits or non-contractual benefits. The employer should be clear in his own mind and then take steps to put the matter plainly to employees. If matters are matters of discretion, each time they are allocated or awarded that discretion should be reconfirmed to the employees specifically.

Interrelation Between Contract and Pension

2.18   Similarly, the interrelation between the contract of employment and the pension fund documentation needs to be considered and analysed. The trustees will very often have an absolute discretion to alter or amend the terms of the pension fund rules and, indeed, the pension fund documentation and the trustees will have a different legal personam from the employer. It may be that it will be the same company but, as trustee, the company will be performing a wholly different function and a fiduciary one. What effect the reservation to the trustees of the right to alter the terms of the pension fund rules at will has upon the contract of employment is a moot point. If the pension fund rules are altered substantially to the employees detriment, could an employee subsequently seek a remedy against either the employer or the pension fund trustee. See further Chapter 10.

Collective Agreements

2.19   In relation to collective agreements, in *The Council of the City of Cardiff* v. *Conde*[2] Mr. Justice Arnold, in the E.A.T., held that if an employment is said to be "subject to nationally negotiated conditions of service," these conditions form part of the contract between the employer and each employee. The same contractual position prevailed in the recent House of Lords case of *Leverton* v. *Clwyd*.[3] In the Cardiff case the relevant part of the letter of appointment read: "The position

---

[2] [1978] I.R.L.R. 218.
[3] [1989] 2 W.L.R. 47.

will be subject to the national scheme of conditions and service prescribed by the National Joint Council for Local Authorities Administrative, Professional, Technical and Clerical Services as supplemented by the Cardiff City Council's own rules and regulations." In *Camden Exhibition and Display Ltd.* v. *Lynott*,[4] working rules laid down by Joint Union Employers Council for the exhibition industry provided that normal working hours were 40 per week and that overtime needed for proper performance of the contract should not be restricted but worked by direct agreement between employer and employees concerned. Statutory statements of particulars were sent to employees which said that hours were in accordance with the working rules. Later several employees resolved to ban overtime. An injunction was granted restraining the employees from breaking their contracts of employment and the employees appealed. The Court of Appeal held that the Employer Council's working rules on overtime were incorporated into the contract.

In *Gibbons* v. *Associated British Ports*,[5] it was held that where a term **2.20** in a collective agreement has been expressly incorporated into an employee's individual contract, that term is not affected by termination of the collective agreement and can only be changed with the employee's consent. The status of collective agreements in relation to the contracts of employment of non-union members is more complex. In *Gray, Dunn & Co. Ltd.* v. *Edwards*,[6] where employers negotiated a detailed agreement with a recognised union, the employers were entitled to assume that all unionised employees knew of and were bound by the provisions of that agreement. Again, in *Land* v. *West Yorkshire Metropolitan County Council*,[7] it was held that where a contract based on a collective agreement is to be varied or terminated, such a change will only bind those who are members of the negotiating union or who accepted the change individually. It is submitted that this must be right and that the relationship between the union and its members creates one of agency pursuant to which the union is entitled to negotiate on behalf of the employee with the employer. By the same token, if an employee is not a member of a union then the union cannot bind the employee.

There is authority for the suggestion that a local agreement provided **2.21** for in a national agreement may amend the national agreement even if there is no formal record of the local agreement's existence and the terms of the local agreement can be presumed from the evidence.

---

[4] [1966] 1 Q.B. 555.
[5] [1985] I.R.L.R. 376.
[6] [1980] I.R.L.R. 23.
[7] [1979] I.C.R. 452.

Again in *Barratt* v. *National Coal Board*,[8] a local arrangement provided for by national agreement can displace the terms of a national agreement incorporated into individual employment contracts, albeit the local arrangement can be informal. Compare this approach with *Gaskoll Conversions Ltd.* v. *Mercer*,[9] in which it was held that a local agreement with no binding force contractually will not vary a national agreement expressed to take precedence over all other national and local agreements.

2.22   In *National Coal Board* v. *National Union of Mineworkers and Others*,[10] it was held in the Chancery Division that a distinction must be drawn between terms which are of their nature apt to become enforceable terms of an individual's contract and those that are not. An agreement providing machinery for collective bargaining and resolving disputes could not conceivably have been intended to be legally enforceable at the suit of an individual worker and was not, therefore, enforceable— whether or not referred to in the individual's contracts. In *Young* v. *Canadian Northern Railway Company*,[11] it was held that where courts are asked to determine if a collective agreement is incorporated into individual contracts so as to create legal obligations, the courts must consider the appropriateness of the agreement's terms for incorporation.

2.23   Finally in this section, the case of *Dall & Others* v. *A. S. Orr*,[12] serves to enforce observations made above about the contractual effect of documents incorporated into the contract by reference. In that case, the court held that in some circumstances courts may construe a works manual as having contractual force.

Equality Clauses

2.24   Employers can find that, notwithstanding they have taken great care to consider precisely what terms and/or documents should be incorporated into the contract of employment, they have other terms deemed to have been imposed upon the contract by statute. The equality clause is an example of such imposition. The Equal Pay Act 1970 confers a right

---

[8] [1978] I.C.R. 1101.
[9] [1974] I.C.R. 420.
[10] [1986] I.R.L.R. 439, I.C.R. 736.
[11] [1931] A.C. 83.
[12] [1980] I.R.L.R. 413.

to assert that the contract of employment contains an equality clause. Section 1(1) implies into every contract of employment at establishments in Great Britain an equality clause. Section 1(2) defines an equality clause to the effect that a woman is provided equal treatment with any man in the same employment who is engaged in work which is like work or which has been rated as equivalent or which is otherwise of equal value. This means that the woman's contractual terms and conditions of employment shall be no less favourable than those of the man and if the man's contract becomes more favourable than the woman's, then by virtue of the equality clause the woman's contract is immediately brought up to the appropriate level, either by modification of the relevant term of her contract of employment or by the insertion of an appropriate term if there was no such term in the first place. Of course the classic example is pay and an alteration to the level of pay does, in theory, operate as an alteration to a term of the contract provided, of course, that the employer has complied with the statutory obligation to set out scales and rates of pay in written statements of terms and conditions of employment. It is an interesting variation to the old doctrine that parties are free to contract in the way that they wish.

Another example of this modern statutory overlay to that Victorian premise can be found in the Transfer of Undertakings (Protection of Employment) Regulations 1981 (see Appendix 9). Regulation 5 provides that a contract which might otherwise have been terminated by a transfer of the business shall have effect after any such transfer, provided it is a relevant transfer, as if originally made between the person employed under the contract and the transferee of the business. This operates as a unilateral alteration to the very basic structure of the contract, in that it substitutes one employer for another by operation of law and without either employer or employee have any right to consent or object. It is interesting that both these provisions derive from European legislation. It is important to appreciate that an equality clause simply modifies the contract, so that if a woman has complaints which go beyond the terms of contract into the realms of sex discrimination, then the remedy lies under the Sex Discrimination Act 1975 rather than under the Equal Pay Act 1970.

Clearly the most significant case of recent times in relation to the equality clause is *Hayward* v. *Cammell Laird*.[13] This case has had a chequered history and is complicated by the fact that the employers did not plead in their defence that there was a genuine material factor, other than sex, justifying any pay differential. They tried to amend in order to introduce this defence but because, at the first hearing they clearly said they were not relying on it, leave was refused. The case

---

[13] [1988] I.R.L.R. 257.

might have been decided differently otherwise. In the event, the main point went all the way to the House of Lords in 1988 after a tribunal had, back in 1984, found that Miss Hayward, a canteen cook, was employed on work of equal value to that of her male comparators employed as painters, thermal insulation engineers and joiners. The employer said that, notwithstanding this, they did not have to pay the same basic wage because, overall, her terms and conditions were not less favourable. She had paid meal breaks for example. The tribunal construed "pay" in the light of Article 119 and the E.A.T. and the Court of Appeal agreed. The House of Lords did not agree. They said that for the purposes of the Equal Pay Act, a woman doing work of equal value to that of a man is entitled to the same basic wage even if her overall package is more favourable than his. The correct approach is to treat the provision in the contract relating to basic pay as a "term" in its own right, term being specifically referred to in section 1(2)(c)(i) of the Equal Pay Act. It was not to be taken as part of a larger "term" embracing all contractual entitlements. If the term as to basic pay is less favourable then it should be increased notwithstanding other more favourable terms. Not suprisingly, this has caused greater concern to employers and the C.B.I. has expressed itself forcefully on the point. The dangers in cost terms of the equalising up of all benefits can readily be seen. It will be interesting to see if there is now a flood of cases or whether the concern to maintain differentials will act as a counter-balance.

Before leaving equality clauses, reference should be made to *Leverton* v. *Clwyd County Council*,[14] the latest authority on "same employment." If an applicant works at a separate establishment a claim can only be brought if both have common terms and conditions. In this case they worked for the same local authority under terms set by the appropriate N.J.C. and although she had different hours of work and holidays she could bring a claim. The House of Lords again overruled the Court of Appeal.

In *Pickstone* v. *Freemans plc*[15] the House of Lords held that a woman was not barred from claiming equal pay for work of *equal value* simply because she was already being paid as much as a man doing the *same work*. They held that, although that was not what the Act said, it was so by reason of Article 119 and Directive 75/117 which are enforceable in the United Kingdom and EEC law prevails where there is a conflict.

---

[14] [1989] 2 W.L.R. 47.
[15] [1988] 3 W.L.R. 265.

Finally, in *Rainey* v. *Greater Glasgow Health Board*[16] the House of Lords, when dealing with 'genuine material difference' as a justification for different pay levels held that the difference must be significant and relevant in all the circumstances including administrative efficiency and economic factors going beyond a personal equation between the applicant and her comparator. This establishes firmly that the market forces argument in relation to differences in pay is available for employers as a defence. However, it needs detailed evidential support to succeed, as Lloyds Bank found recently in a case in which the Industrial Tribunal held that secretaries were entitled to pay equal to that of messengers. The argument based on *Reed* v. *Booze* that historic wage bargaining arrangements constituted a defence did not avail the Bank and the Tribunal set a fairly high evidential burden on them. The Bank could not meet that burden but will no doubt appeal.

---

[16] [1987] I.R.L.R. 26.

CHAPTER 3

TERMS AND CONDITIONS

Introduction—Types of Terms—Express Terms

Terms and conditions of a contract of employment are usually express **3.1**
in that they are agreed between the parties or representatives of the
parties. They may be agreed orally or in writing.

Terms may also be implied by law or custom and practice. Implied
terms may arise out of the very nature of the contract of employment, for
example, good faith. Another instance is *BAC* v. *Austin*,[1] where the
E.A.T. held, albeit *obiter*, that:

> "it must ordinarily be an implied term of the contract of employment that
> employers do not behave in any way which is intolerable or in a way which
> employees cannot be expected to put up with any longer."

Terms may also be implied by reason of the circumstances surrounding the creation or operation of the contract as opposed to its very
nature.

Other terms are imposed upon the contractual relationship by statute
or by EEC legislation. This chapter deals with the different types of
terms, the next explores variation to those terms.

The obligation to provide written particulars for certain essential terms
and conditions of the employment and the distinction between the

---

[1] [1978] I.R.L.R. 334.

TERMS AND CONDITIONS

written statement and the contract of employment have already been dealt with in Chapter 1. The written statement is not necessarily conclusive of the terms and conditions of the employment, neither does it create a written contract. Clearly, however, it is strong evidence of the terms and conditions of the contract of employment to the extent of the particulars provided. As has been said, however, it is important to set out clearly in writing what are the full terms and conditions of the contract of employment. In addition, employers will want express terms dealing with matters such as confidentiality, possible restrictive covenants, terms relating to solicitation of business and employees in the event of termination and other terms that will relate to the particular employment. For example, broking houses will wish to incorporate express dealing rules, banks will want to incorporate express terms dealing with the proper conduct of employees' finances and so forth.

3.2 The following terms may need to be covered expressly in a standard contract of employment, although different degrees of detail will be relevant for different types of employment:

(1) Name of employer and employee
(2) Job title
(3) Place of work and mobility obligation, if any
(4) Start date and any provision as to continuous employment
(5) Pay
(6) Hours of work and overtime
(7) Holidays
(8) Absence, sick pay and Statutory Sick Pay
(9) Medical examinations—Access to Medical Reports (Appendix 3)
(10) Notice periods
(11) Pension provision and retirement age
(12) Grievance procedure
(13) Disciplinary procedure
(14) Health and safety
(15) Duty of confidence
(16) Provisions in relation to employers' property
[(17) Equal opportunity policy statement—this may well be in a rule or handbook]
(18) Provision as to variation
(19) Reference to any external documentation also to be incorporated within the contract or not, as the case may be
(20) Covenants and restrictions

3.3 The express terms will need to be agreed to by the employee as will any subsequent alteration to express terms.

3.4 Set out in Appendix 4 is a check list and specimen framework for a general form of contract of employment.

Implied Terms

Tests of implied terms

It is not open to the courts to imply a term into a contract just because **3.5** it may be reasonable so to do. Lord Justice Scrutton in 1918 said in *Reigate* v. *Union Manufacturing Co.*,[2]

> "The first thing is to see what the parties have expressed in the contract; and then an implied term is not to be added because the court thinks it would have been reasonable to have inserted it in the contract. A term can only be implied if it is necessary in the business sense to give efficacy to the contract; that is, if it is such a term that it can confidently be said that if at the time the contract was being negotiated someone had said to the parties, 'What will happen in such a case,' they would both have replied, 'Of course, so and so will happen; we did not trouble to say that; it is too clear.' Unless the court comes to such a conclusion as that, it ought not to imply a term which the parties themselves have not expressed."

It is suggested that this concept has been substantially eroded by **3.6** Industrial Tribunals and the body of case law that has built up under the unfair dismissal provisions of the last 20 years. Indeed, the implication of terms was given an added impetus by the strict construction of the Court of Appeal in *Western Excavating* v. *Sharp*,[3] (see paras. 5.1 and 5.81 below) in constructive dismissal cases. In this case the Court of Appeal said that a contractual test was appropriate, not one of reasonableness. A constructive dismissal only arises where there has been a breach of a fundamental term, not where the employer has behaved unreasonably. Tribunals have more frequently tended to high-light implied terms subsequent to that case and to find that the breach of those terms can give rise to a constructive dismissal. The *B.A.C.* v. *Austin* (see para. 3.1) case is one in point, although the E.A.T. did go on to say that they would not wish tribunals to guide themselves other than in accordance with *Western Excavating*.

---

[2] [1918] 1 K.B. 592 at p. 605.
[3] [1978] I.C.R. 221.

TERMS AND CONDITIONS

In *Woods* v. *W.M. Car Services (Peterborough) Ltd.*[4] Lord Denning said that,

> "It is the duty of the employer to be good and considerate to his servants (sic). Just as an employee can be guilty of misconduct justifying dismissal, so an employer can be guilty of misconduct justifying the employee in leaving at once without notice."

This may be, however, a good example of an implication by reason of the very essence of the relationship rather than what Lord Justice Scrutton had in mind.

In *Lewis* v. *Motorworld Garages Ltd.*[5] the Court of Appeal held that the tribunal had erred in law in finding that the employee had not shown that the employer had breached the implied term of his contract that they should not undermine the relationship of trust and confidence which ought to subsist between employer and employee. Lord Justice Glidewell put the matter very clearly:

> "The principles to be found in the relevant authorities can, I believe, be summarised as follows:
> (a)   In order to prove that he has suffered constructive dismissal, an employee who leaves his employment must prove that he did so as the result of a breach of contract by his employer, which shows that the employer no longer intends to be bound by an essential term of the contract: *Western Excavating Limited* v. *Sharp.*[6]
> (b)   However, there are normally implied in a contract of employment mutual rights and obligations of trust and confidence. A breach of this implied term may justify the employee in leaving and claiming he has been constructively dismissed: see *Post Office* v. *Roberts*[7] and *Woods* v. *W.M. Car Services Ltd.*[8]
> (c)   The breach of this implied obligation of trust and confidence may consist of a series of actions on the part of the employer which cumulatively amount to a breach of the term, though each individual incident may not do so. In particular, in such a case the last action of the employer which leads to the employee leaving need not itself be a breach of contract; the question is, does the cumulative series of acts taken together amount to a breach of the implied term? see *Woods* v. *W.M. Car Services Ltd.*[9] This is the 'last straw' situation.

---

[4] [1982] I.R.L.R. 413.
[5] [1985] I.R.L.R. 465.
[6] [1978] I.R.L.R. 27.
[7] [1980] I.R.L.R. 347.
[8] [1981] I.R.L.R. 347 *per* Browne Wilkinson J. at 350.
[9] [1981] I.R.L.R. 173.

(d) The decision whether there has been a breach of contract by the employer so as to constitute constructive dismissal of the employee is one of mixed law and fact for the Industrial Tribunal. An appellate court, whether the Employment Appeal Tribunal or the Court of Appeal, may only overrule that decision if the Tribunal has misdirected itself as to the relevant law or has made a finding of fact for which there is no supporting evidence or which no reasonable Tribunal could make: see *Pedersen* v. *Camden L.B.C.*[10] and *Woods* v. *W.M. Car Services Ltd.* applying the test laid down in *Edwards* v. *Bairstow.*"[11]

In *Shirlaw* v. *Southern Foundries Ltd.*[12] it was held by the Court of **3.7** Appeal in 1939 that it was open to a court to imply a term into a contract where it was so obvious that both parties treated it as "going without saying." In the case, Mr. Shirlaw was appointed managing director of Southern Foundries on a 10 year fixed term contract. Note that a 10 year fixed term contract is unacceptable now, one to three years being usual and five a statutory maximum for company directors. The articles of association of the company provided that the managing director should be subject to the same provisions as to removal and resignation as those applicable to other directors, but those provisions were nonetheless subject to Mr. Shirlaw's contract of employment or service contract with Southern Foundries. There was a takeover and Southern Foundries gave the acquiring company the power to remove from office any director of Southern Foundries. In due course, the acquiring company removed Mr. Shirlaw from his post as managing director and his appointment was terminated. On the claim for damages for wrongful dismissal Mr. Shirlaw contended that there was an implied term to the effect that Southern Foundries would not create a right whereby he could be removed from his office as director. The Court of Appeal, albeit by a majority, upheld this argument. The Court of Appeal said that if at the start of the 10 year contract Shirlaw and Southern Foundries had been asked whether Southern Foundries could create a situation which would enable them to remove Shirlaw from his directorship, then their answer would have been, of course, "No." This was because Shirlaw was employed on a fixed term contract and he had agreed not to engage in the restricted activities beyond the end of the term of that contract. The court did, nonetheless, acknowledge that the recognition of an implied term in a written contract is a matter that must be exercised with some care and that courts are too often invited to do so

---

[10] [1982] I.R.L.R. 413.
[11] [1956] A.C. 14.
[12] [1939] 2 A.E.R. 113.

upon vague and uncertain grounds. It may be that the Courts and tribunals still have this in mind in implying terms that arise from circumstance or a particular contract. However, I believe that the tendency to imply terms which some would say are merely statements of hitherto unspoken concepts on which the very nature of the relationship is founded does deviate from the basic contractual norm that implied terms should only be introduced into contracts where the officious bystander would say, "Oh yes, of course" when asked whether a particular term should be included. The bystander might not say trust and confidence is a term but rather an abstract concept not to be formulated. As indicated above, however, the implication of such terms interestingly derives mainly from constructive dismissal law, and largely after *Western Excavating*, and later *Essex County Council* (below).

3.8   In *O'Brien* v. *Associated Fire Alarms Ltd.*,[13] the Court of Appeal said that the existence and extent of implied terms are questions of law with which appellate courts are entitled to interfere.

There has been an interesting battle between the tribunals and the higher courts as to the extent to which the higher courts are entitled to interfere in decisions of lower courts. The E.A.T. in particular has tried consistently to set itself up as being the appellate industrial jury court and, it seems, slightly resents the restraining influence put upon the industrial common sense exercised in that court by the Court of Appeal. The general perception is that the Court of Appeal has exercised a restraint upon the E.A.T. and the industrial tribunals by adopting a stricter and more "contractual" approach to various industrial issues. In *Woods* v. *W.M. Car Services*[14] the Court of Appeal said that the E.A.T. should *only* interfere with a decision of an Industrial Tribunal if it misdirected itself in law or it was so unreasonable that no reasonable tribunal could reach that decision. The E.A.T. ought not to interfere merely because it would have reached a different conclusion.

3.9   In *Lake* v. *Essex County Council*,[15] the Court of Appeal (Lord Denning presiding) held that in circumstances where the employee's contract allowed her over three hours as a part time teacher to do her marking and preparation work, those extra hours were a voluntary act and were so unpredictable that they could not be regarded as contractual. It appeared that although, under her contract, three hours 40 minutes of the hours per week were time during which she was not teaching and it was envisaged that she would do all necessary marking and

---

[13] [1968] 1 W.L.R. 1916.
[14] *Supra*.
[15] [1979] I.C.R. 577 and I.R.L.R. 241.

preparation in that time, she nonetheless worked at home for several hours extra to prepare for classes. The employers defended the unfair dismissal claim on the basis that she did not work under a contract which normally involved 21 or more hours per week and that the employee could not, therefore, accumulate the requisite number of weeks service to claim unfair dismissal rights. She could only succeed if she could establish that it was an implied term in her contract that she was required to do extra work in the preparation of lessons, etc. The tribunal found there was no such implied term but the E.A.T. allowed her appeal. The Court of Appeal reversed the E.A.T.'s finding and restored the finding that there was no such implied term. They said that applying the established principles for implying contractual terms, it seemed that her employers would not have agreed to such a term. In addition, it was too vague because the employers were unable to supervise or measure the extra work for the purposes of payment. Indeed, the Court of Appeal went on to say that neither could such implied term be inferred on grounds of business efficacy, nor would the answer of the officious bystander have been that an implied term should have been incorporated in the contract.

Interestingly, in *Mears* v. *Safecar Security Ltd.*[16] the Court of Appeal **3.10** said that it is open to tribunals to imply as an agreed term a term which would not have been assented to at once by both parties at the time when the contract was formed. Such a course should only be adopted where the evidence shows that one party would have agreed to the term straight away and, although the other would not have initially agreed, he would have eventually assented to it once he realised there would be no contract otherwise. This case is of particular interest in relation to sick pay. The Court of Appeal said that it could not be said that as a general rule, as a legal incident of a contract of employment, there should be no sick pay. Indeed, the contrary applies. There has been a controversy about whether or not, if a contract is silent as to sick pay, sick pay should automatically be implied. In that case, the tribunal had presumed that he was entitled to sick pay unless his employers could prove to the contrary. The tribunal majority applying the traditional business efficacy and officious bystander tests held that the presumption had not been rebutted. Both the E.A.T. and the Court of Appeal said that tribunals had to ascertain the appropriate implied term by looking at all the surrounding circumstances and without any legal presumption of entitlement to sick pay. On the facts of the case, the company never paid sick pay to anyone and would not have made an exception for this particular employee. The tribunal found as a fact that he would have eventually taken the job once he realised that, unless he agreed that he

---

[16] [1982] I.C.R. 626.

would get no sick pay, the offer would have been withdrawn. Quite apart from its implications in relation to implied terms, this case is important for sick pay purposes since there is very often an assumption that, if a contract is silent as to sick pay, sick pay will be paid. Clearly it is a matter of investigating the facts and circumstances in relation to that particular employment and that particular company's practices before anyone can conclude whether or not sick pay is to be paid.

Implied Terms of Trust and Confidence

3.11 As indicated above, the area where implied terms are now creating the most interest is in the area of implied terms as to support for employees and trust and confidence. One sees the beginnings of this in *Giblin* v. *Seismograph Services (England) Ltd.*[17] where it was held that the employer's conduct up to the time when their alleged repudiation had been accepted, was relevant in deciding whether or not they had broken an implied term not to behave intolerably. In *Fyfe and McGrougher* v. *Byrne*[18] it was held that neither wilful nor negligent conduct on the part of the employers could, in the circumstances give rise to an intolerable state of affairs entitling an employee to claim constructive dismissal.

3.12 *Robinson* v. *Crompton Parkinson Ltd.*[19] is perhaps the base case for the trust and confidence argument. In that case it was held by Mr. Justice Kilner Brown that in all employment contracts there is an implied term that the employer will not do anything which will undermine mutual trust and confidence. The term can be broken where an employer accuses an employee of dishonesty in circumstances where there is no basis for the accusation. In the particular case the tribunal had not considered whether the employers had any basis for their accusation but merely dealt with the case on the basis that the employee had taken umbrage too soon. It is with respect suggested that this case does reflect E.A.T. thinking. Further, it must be clear that it is important that there is mutual trust and confidence between employer and employee. Mutuality of trust and confidence is important in that, if employers rely upon the breaking of that degree of trust on the part of the employee to found action on their part, then why should the same right not be

---

[17] Unreported: E.A.T. 305/78.
[18] [1977] I.R.L.R. 29.
[19] [1978] I.R.L.R. 61.

available to an employee. In *Masso* v. *Warham*,[20] the implied term of mutual trust and confidence was broken where the employer, who had previously given a favourable reference, referred an incident to the police without any prior notification to the employee. The police eventually decided not to prosecute. The employee resigned and was successful in a constructive dismissal case by reason of the employer's failure to discuss the matter first with the employee. In *Post Office* v. *Roberts*[21] it was held that the implied term of mutual trust and confidence can be broken even though the employers did not intend their behaviour to have that effect.

Other Implied Terms

As suggested above, although these cases may provide useful **3.13** protection for employees, they may be statements reflecting the essence of the employment relationship classified as implied terms by tribunals. Apart from the implied term of trust and confidence, there are many other terms that tribunals and courts have sought to imply into contracts. In 1930 the House of Lords confirmed that where one of the benefits derived by an employee from employment is the publicity which goes with performing the job, then it is an implied term of the contract that he will be provided with work—actors fall within the category. The House of Lords held in 1937 that where the parties to an employment contract failed to agree the remuneration payable to the employee, it was open to the court to imply a term that the employee would be entitled to a "reasonable remuneration." When ascertaining this figure, the courts are entitled to have regard to the previous conversations between the parties as to the value put each upon the employees services. Perhaps the area that is most difficult nowadays is that in relation to the implied period of notice if the contract is silent as to notice. In relation to directors of companies, the range is perhaps between six and 18 months. Some would say that is a little on the top heavy side in the current climate and that a year is a maximum period of reasonable implied notice for a director.

---

[20] Unreported: E.A.T. 194/81.
[21] [1980] I.R.L.R. 347.

TERMS AND CONDITIONS

Implied Duty of Confidentiality

3.14   In relation to the implied obligations of confidentiality, *Faccenda Chicken* v. *Fowler*[22] is one of the key cases. Mr. Justice Goulding's judgment at first instance contained some useful guidelines which were somewhat altered by the Court of Appeal, who said, in relation to confidential information, that in the absence of express terms, an employee is bound by his implied duty of good faith to his employer not to use or disclose for the duration of his employment confidential information gained in the course of his employment, and was furthermore bound by an implied term not to use or disclose trade secrets either during *or after* employment. There is no implied term imposing a post termination obligation not to use confidential information short of a trade secret. The sales information, and that relating to prices in this instance, did not amount to trade secrets and the employees were at liberty to use and disclose the information after they had left the plaintiffs' employment. Interestingly, they overruled Mr. Justice Goulding by holding that an employer cannot extend by restrictive covenant the period of protection for confidential information of the category that is only protected during employment by an express term. A covenant will only be enforced if the protection sought is reasonably necessary to protect a trade secret or prevent some personal influence over customers being abused in order to entice them away. The Court did say, however, that innumerable pieces of information are capable of being trade secrets and what is or is not is a matter of evidence in each case.

See also Chapter 6 paragraph 6.116 below.

3.15   *Hivac Ltd.* v. *Park Royal Scientific Instruments Ltd.*[23] is one of the leading cases on the subject. It has been referred to in so many cases since that perhaps one does not need to refer to it now, save to say that where a skilled employee works in his spare time for a competitor, there is a prima facie breach of an implied contractual term of good faith and fidelity to the employer which can be restrained by injunction. In *Lion Laboratories Ltd.* v. *Evans and Others*[24] the Court of Appeal ruled that an employee is under an implied obligation not to disclose information received in confidence and can be restrained by injunction from so doing.

3.16   Care needs to be taken by the employer to cover what should be covered. Express term can very often be preferable to leaving the matter to implication. In *United Indigo Chemical Company Ltd.* v.

---

[22] [1986] I.C.R. 297.
[23] [1946] C.L. 169.
[24] [1985] Q.B. 526.

Robinson[25] in the Chancery Division in 1931 it was held that there is no implied term that an ex-employee will not use knowledge honestly acquired during his employment when no warning as to secrecy was given. In *Faccenda Chicken* v. *Fowler* (see above) again it was clear that the implied obligation not to disclose information learned during employment in competition after leaving will cover only highly confidential information amounting to trade secrets.

Duty to Account for Secret Profits

Another fundamental concept in relation to contracts of employment **3.17** which derives perhaps from the law of agency and which is, again, an essential part of the employment relationship relates to accounting for secret profits. *Boston Deep Sea Fishing and Ice Company* v. *Ansell*.[26] The managing director was dismissed. In the course of his dealings he had come by certain secret profits, that is to say commission on contracts to build a number of fishing smacks for the company and bonuses in respect of certain services supplied by the company to two companies in which he was, in fact, a shareholder. It was held that the managing director must account to the company for the bonuses received. It was contrary to equity that the agent or the servant should retain money so received without the knowledge of his master. The law "implies a use, that is to say, there is an implied contract, if you put it as a legal proposition—there is an equitable right, if you treat it as a matter of equity—as between the principal and agent that the agent should pay it over, which renders the agent liable to be sued for money had and received, and the equitable right in the master to receive it, and to take it out of the hands of the agent, which gives the principal a right to relief in equity." The liability to an account for the commission, as opposed to the bonus, had not been seriously disputed and there was no appeal on that point.

Industrial Action and Implied Terms

One of the important implied term cases in relation to working **3.18** practices was *Secretary of State for Employment* v. *A.S.L.E.F. (No. 2)*.[27]

---

[25] [1931] 49 R.P.C. 178.
[26] [1888] 39 Ch.D. 339.
[27] [1972] Q.B. 455.

TERMS AND CONDITIONS

In this case the executive committees of the three railway unions instructed their members to work strictly to rule. Under the Industrial Relations Act 1971, the Secretary of State applied to the Industrial Court for an order for a ballot of the unions' members. It was necessary for the Secretary of State to show that the activities of the railway workers were "carried on in breach of their contracts of employment." The Industrial Court ordered the ballot and the Court of Appeal dismissed the unions' appeal. Lord Denning, presiding, said that the meaning of the instruction to work to rule was not in doubt and it was intended to mean, and understood to mean, "Keep the rules of your employment to the very letter, but, whilst doing so, do your very utmost to disrupt the undertaking." He posed the question whether that was a breach of contract. He agreed that an employee is not bound positively to do more for his employer than required by contract, but went on to say that what the employee must not do is wilfully obstruct the employer as he goes about his business. Lord Denning was suggesting that there is an implied term not wilfully to prevent the carrying out of the contract. Sir John Donaldson then in the National Industrial Relations Court had referred to "the fundamental obligation of every employee to behave fairly to his employer and to do a fair days work."

Although *Miles* v. *Wakefield Metropolitan District Council*[28] is not an implied term case it is an interesting up to date version of "limited industrial action," which went to the House of Lords. The Registrar of Weddings was taking industrial action and refusing to conduct weddings on Saturdays. The employers required full performance of the duties and refused to pay for part performance. The applicant was in fact carrying out some Saturday duties but the employer refused to pay for the whole of Saturday during the currency of the industrial dispute. It was held that the employer was entitled to refuse to accept partial performance of contractual duties where the employee refuses to carry out the full range of those duties as a form of industrial action. Where the employer makes it clear that he will not accept partial performance, the employee is not entitled to be paid even for those services which he does perform since he will be unable to aver that he was willing to perform full extent of his duties in accordance with the contract. There was a subsidiary point as to whether the salary was remuneration or an honorarium for the holding of an office but that is not material for these purposes. The central point for present purposes was that where an employee refuses as a form of industrial action to perform his full contractual duties but offers partial performance, the employer can

---

[28] [1987] I.R.L.R. 193.

choose whether or not to accept the partial performance. It is submitted however that the way in which the employer communicates the non-acceptance of partial performance and structures the deduction of pay is important. The employer must avoid taking any action which could be said to constitute a repudiation of the contract on the part of the employer notwithstanding breaches by the employee. In *Willuszynski* v. *London Borough of Tower Hamlets*,[29] the Court of Appeal overruled the Judge at first instance. The facts were that the employer informed an employee that partial performance of his contract due to industrial action was unacceptable and he would not be paid. The employee continued to perform the substantial part of his contractual duties and his superior continued to give him instructions in respect of those duties. The Judge held that on the clear facts of the case the defendants were not entitled to withhold the whole of the plaintiff's pay for the relevant period. It might be that they would have been entitled to withhold two and a half or three hours pay (being the time which would have been spent on various matters) but that was not pleaded. The Judge acknowledged that it was a fundamental duty of an employee to comply with instructions given within the scope of his contract of employment but held that the breach was minimal, not affecting the conscious performance of the plaintiff's duties in all respects save in one particular issue as to the answering of members' enquiries. The Court of Appeal said that in their view *Miles* v. *Wakefield* (see above) establishes that an employee is not entitled to remuneration under the contract of employment unless he is willing to perform that contract. They did not think that they were dealing with any question of an application of the doctrine of "substantial performance." The case was not concerned with entire contracts. They did not accept the breach was insubstantial. In a telling passage Lord Justice Fox said:

"The plaintiff was in breach of his own obligations; he was not willing to comply, and did not comply, with the contract. He was not, therefore, entitled to sue for payment. That is simply the consequences of the principle stated in *Miles* v. *Wakefield*."

It is interesting that the employer had made it clear that, if the employee was not prepared to comply with his contract, then he was not required to work, and that if he did work he did so voluntarily and that he would not be paid. The question of a lock out was mentioned

---

[29] C.A., April 26, 1989, T.L.R. May 1989.

and it is submitted that employers must be careful to understand and appreciate when action of this sort can lead them into the imposition of a lock out which has rather different consequences. A lock out in the instant case was impractical since some of the staff were working quite normally and in accordance with their contracts. The Court of Appeal decided that it was reasonable in the circumstances for the employer to allow the staff in dispute to come and go as they wished. Lord Justice Nicholls said:

> "In my view, the defendant was entitled to adopt the stance that, so long as the plaintiff continued to refuse to carry out part of his contractual duties, the defendant would not accept his services and the plaintiff would not be paid. . . . The plaintiff's considered statement that he would not discharge this part of his duties was, in law, a repudiatory breach of his contract . . . entitling the defendant to . . . dismiss the plaintiff. . . . In my view, however, termination of the contract is not the only remedy available to an employer in such circumstances. . . . The employer is entitled . . . to decline to accept the proffered partial performance. He can hold himself out as continuing to be ready and willing to carry out the contract of employment, and to accept from the employee work as agreed and to pay him for that work as agreed, while declining to accept or pay for part only of the agreed work."

Terms Implied by Custom and Practice

3.19   Certain terms can be implied by custom and practice. In *Scott* v. *Victor Blagden (Barking) Ltd.*,[30] Scott was employed as a maintenance fitter. He was dismissed for refusing to come into work on Sunday January 3, 1982 to do some maintenance work. The factory had closed down for the Christmas break but it was essential that the work was carried out before production staff returned. He was dismissed and claimed compensation for unfair dismissal. The main argument centred on whether or not he was contractually obliged to work on the day in question since it fell within the holiday. He candidly admitted that it had been the practice over the years that major maintenance would be carried out at weekends and that he had in the past come in during the summer shutdown. The employer said that this amounted to an implied contractual term, but he said that it did not cover statutory holiday periods. The tribunal accepted the employer's view, as did the E.A.T.

---

[30] Unreported: E.A.T. 367/82.

The E.A.T. said there was evidence to support the tribunal's finding that it was a term of his contract implied by custom and practice that he would be required to do maintenance work at weekends and during factory shutdowns.

A term can only be implied by virtue of custom on the grounds that it **3.20** is certain and "notorious" the burden of proving the existence of an implied term rests with the party to the contract who alleges the existence of the term.

There are many other examples of implied terms operating between **3.21** the parties in relation to contracts and it is not particularly instructive to list them all, save to say that one needs to take great care in making an assertion that something is in breach of contract or, rather, is not in breach of contract without first considering whether the matter complained of could not constitute an implied term of contract.

CHAPTER 4

VARIATION

Since a contract of employment governs the relationship between an **4.1**
employer and an employee sometimes for many years, its terms often
change. For instance an employee joining a company as a school
leaver and leaving on retirement as a member of senior management
will not' have been employed throughout on the same terms. Most
variations come about by mutual agreement—employees seldom if ever
refuse a pay rise or promotion. However, occasions may arise when,
normally the employer, may wish to vary the terms of employment not
necessarily to the benefit of the employee but for economic or organisational reasons. This chapter examines when an employer can vary the
terms of the contract of employment and when he cannot and, where
there is no express or implied right to vary the terms to what extent and
how he can go about unilaterally imposing new terms on the workforce.

The Right to Vary

Express right

The express right is perhaps most frequently found in, and best **4.2**
exemplified by, contracts of employment which contain mobility or
flexibility clauses by virtue of which the employer expressly reserves the
right to require the employee to carry out his or her duties at a different
location or reserves the right to alter those duties. Thus for instance in

VARIATION

Parry v. *Holst & Company Ltd.*[1] the court held that where the employee's contract provided that "an operative may be transferred at any time during the period of his employment from one job to another" when the employee refused to transfer from one site to another and was consequently dismissed he was not entitled to a redundancy payment. Similarly in *I.C.I. Ltd.* v. *McCallum*[2] where the contract provided that the employers were entitled, at their discretion, to transfer the employee from one operation to another carrying a higher or lower rate of pay, and the employee refused to be so tranferred and left, his claim for a redundancy payment failed. The court held that there had been no termination but simply a transfer within the existing contractual terms.

Dismissals and the "Reasonableness" Obligation—Section 57(3) E.P.C.A.

4.3   However, whilst a clearly drafted mobility or flexibility clause will defeat a claim for a redundancy payment following a transfer, the position is not quite so clear cut if the employee decides to claim unfair dismissal. If the employee resigns and seeks to claim constructive dismissal the employer will normally be successful in opposing the claim since if there has been no breach by him of the contractual terms, he will not be found to have dismissed the employee. If instead the employer takes the initiative and dismisses the employee for refusing to transfer location or perform alternative duties, the dismissal will be clear and the Tribunal will have to be satisfied that the employer acted reasonably in dismissing the employee (see section 57(3) E.P.C.A.). Consequently it is not sufficient for the employer simply to rely on the mobility or flexibility obligation in the contract and dismiss if the employee refuses to comply with that obligation when required to do so. The employer must also consider for instance whether the employee has domestic commitments which make it difficult or impossible for him to comply with the mobility or flexibility obligation and whether these can be in some way accommodated in order not to fall foul of the "reasonableness" requirement of section 57(3) E.P.C.A.

---

[1] [1968] I.T.R. 317.
[2] [1969] I.T.R. 24.

Ambiguous Clauses

Even where the employer has an express right to vary, he must **4.4**
nonetheless ensure that the proposed variation is within the limits of the
contract. A clear and unambiguous mobility or flexibility obligation
should present little difficulty for an employer, for example in *Parry* v.
Holst & Co. Ltd. (see above) the court rejected the employee's
submission that the mobility requirement should be limited to a place of
work within a reasonable travelling distance from the employee's home.
The words of the contractual term were clear and simple and there was
little room for implying any qualification. However, should the clause
relied on prove to be ambiguous, there is a general rule that the
ambiguity will be construed against the party relying on it. Consequently
an employer seeking to rely on an ambiguous mobility or flexibility
obligation will find the courts will interpret it in the way least favourable
to the employer.

Drafting Flexibility Clauses

Drafting a clear and unambiguous mobility clause is not difficult, but **4.5**
the same may not be said for a flexibility obligation. Consequently an
obligation to perform duties other than those for which the employee
was originally employed is likely to be construed by reference to the
general parameters of the job title and whilst the employer may be
entitled to require the employee to carry out different duties, the nature
of those duties would have to remain the same. In *Peter Carnie & Son* v.
Paton[3] the E.A.T. found that an employee who was engaged to do
unskilled general duties of various kinds could not claim that his
employers had repudiated his contract after they no longer required him
to perform that part of his duties which he liked most. In that case Mr.
Paton was employed in a garage doing "general garage duties/stores".
During the early part of his employment he performed a variety of duties
many of them being of a general handyman nature. However when the
employers expanded their car hire business Mr. Paton became more
involved with this aspect and in particular the reception side of car hire

---

[3] [1979] I.R.L.R. 260, E.A.T.

work. Immediately before his resignation in addition to his general handyman duties he spent 75 per cent. of his time on car hire work and 25 per cent. related to the reception side of the car hire work. Because they were not satisfied with his performance on the reception side his employers informed him that he should carry out all his former functions except those on the reception side of the car hire business. Mr. Paton resigned claiming he had been constructively and unfairly dismissed. In allowing the employer's appeal from a finding of unfair dismissal by the tribunal, the E.A.T. held, *inter alia*, that Mr. Paton was engaged to do a variety of unskilled duties of a general nature. This inevitably envisaged that these duties might be altered from time to time to meet the changing needs of the business and it was wrong to suggest that in this case the removal of one aspect of his duties amounted to a repudiatory breach of contract. (See also *Roberts and Howells* v. *Firth Cleveland Engineering Ltd.*, Chapter 5 para. 5.25 in relation to suitable alternative work and "guarantee payments".)

4.6 By contrast, in *Joseph Steinfeld & Co. Ltd.* v. *Reypert*[4] the E.A.T. came to a different conclusion when an employee appointed as a "Sales Manager (Sales Director Designate)" was given no duties of a managerial nature. This amounted to a breach of contract entitling the employee to claim constructive dismissal. The essential test will be "what was the employee employed to do".

This should not stop employers providing suitably drafted 'flexibility' clauses in contracts where appropriate. At the very least such clauses provide a lever or focus for implementing some flexibility.

Implied right

4.7 As indicated above there are two main legal tests for implying terms into contracts:

(a) are they so obvious that it would go without saying and the parties would have agreed to them?
(b) are they necessary to give business efficacy to the contract?

Applying these tests it may be possible for an employer to show that whilst there was not reserved by the contract any express right to vary, there is nonetheless an implied right to vary one or more of the terms of

---

[4] Unreported: E.A.T. 550/78.

the contract. It is again primarily in the areas of mobility and flexibility of duties that the courts have in certain circumstances been prepared to imply a right to vary so as to entitle an employer to change the employee's place of work or his duties.

The Officious Bystander Test

The general principles as to when a term will be implied by reason of **4.8** business efficacy or, by, as it is commonly known, the "officious bystander" test, is dealt with in more detail above (see Chapter 3). However, as a general reminder in *Shirlaw* v. *(1) Southern Foundries Ltd. and (2) Federated Foundries Ltd.*[5] the Court of Appeal held that in relation to the officious bystander test terms could only be implied into the contract where "if, while the parties were making their bargain, an officious bystander were to suggest some express provision for it in their agreement, they would testily suppress him with a common 'oh, of course.' "

The Business Efficacy Test

It is however the business efficacy test which is most likely to be **4.9** applied where an employer is seeking to argue an implied right to vary. Examples of the cases in which the courts have and have not implied a contractual right to vary may assist in illustrating the application of the principle. For instance in *Burnett* v. *F.A. Hughes & Co. Ltd.*[6] a salesman whose sales territory was changed could not claim constructive dismissal because there was an implied term in his contract that he should be responsible for such areas as his employers should reasonably require. Similarly in *Jones* v. *Associated Tunnelling Co. Ltd.*[7] the E.A.T. concluded that the employee, a tunneller working on contracts at NCB collieries, could be required to work at any place within reasonable daily reach of his home. In the more recent decision in *McAndrew* v.

---

[5] [1939] 2 All E.R. 113.
[6] Unreported: E.A.T. 109/77.
[7] [1981] I.R.L.R. 477.

Prestwick Circuits Ltd.[8] the E.A.T. held that where the applicant employee was told to alter his place of work the next working day to another factory owned by the employer 15 miles away, he had been unfairly constructively dismissed. Both the tribunal and the E.A.T. did however hold that there was to be implied into his contract a mobility clause, but only within a reasonable distance and on reasonable notice. Consequently it was the employer's failure to give reasonable notice of the variation which led to the fundamental breach.

Consensual or other types of variation

4.10   In the absence of any express or implied right to vary the terms of the contract the parties are still at liberty to agree to a variation of the terms and this agreement may come about in a number of ways. The agreement to the variation itself may be express or implied.

Express

4.11   Express agreement needs little explanation. As with the contract itself, the agreed variation may be in writing or oral.

Implied

4.12   The circumstances in which agreement to a variation will be implied need some further examination.

By Conduct

Where, after having been notified of a proposed variation in terms of the contract of employment, the employee continues to work in accord-

---

[8] [1988] I.R.L.R. 514.

ance with the terms of the amended contract, then, generally, he will be taken to have agreed to that variation. However, the position is not quite so clear where the variation has no immediate effect on the terms under which the employee works and he simply stays silent. Whilst the employee's conduct and failure to object may amount to implied agreement to the variation in his terms, the E.A.T. has held that this view should be adopted with caution and mainly in respect of terms, for instance pay, where the change is of immediate effect. Consequently in *Jones* v. *Associated Tunnelling Co. Ltd.*[9] Mr. Jones was first employed as a tunneller with a firm of contractors for the N.C.B. and nothing was said about his being transferred to other collieries. His written statement of terms of employment was silent on the matter. Five years after the commencement of his employment he was transferred to a new colliery and did not object. Some four years later he was given another statement of terms of employment which expressly stated that he could be transferred to any site of his employer's choosing. A yet further statement issued a further three years later said much the same thing and Mr. Jones did not object to either of these at the time. His employers subsequently ordered him to transfer to a colliery nearby whereupon he resigned claiming this change in his workplace entitled him to treat himself as constructively dismissed and entitled to a redundancy payment. The industrial tribunal rejected his claim on the grounds that he had, by not objecting to the earlier written statements agreed to a variation of his contract. Thus there was no breach of contract which could give rise to a constructive dismissal claim. Although the E.A.T. dismissed the employee's appeal on different grounds they disapproved the tribunal's finding of acquiescence to the variation and held, albeit obiter, that to imply an agreement on the facts was not appropriate. What they did imply was a mobility term. The Court of Appeal also did so in *Courtaulds Northern Spinning Ltd.* v. *Sibson.*[10] At term could be implied that the employee could be transferred to work at by a different route. It is clear, however, that implying an agreement on the part of an employee by a different route, implying an agreement on the part of an employee to vary the terms of his employment is a course which should be adopted with great caution.

A distinction should be made between matters which are of immedi- **4.13** ate practical application where absence of protest may well be taken to be implied agreement and those matters which are not. The E.A.T. thought it unrealistic to require an employee to risk confrontation with his

---

[9] [1981] I.R.L.R. 477.
[10] [1988] I.C.R. 451.

VARIATION

employer on a matter such as that in the instant case which had no immediate practical impact on him. Reliance on an employee's agreement being implied by his tacit acceptance particularly where the variation does not have immediate effect is also from an evidential point of view a dangerous course. The employer's position will remain uncertain until he seeks to enforce the term as varied, at which stage the employee could deny his acceptance of the variation not only on the basis of the dicta in the above case, but also by questioning whether he was in fact ever made properly aware of the variation. Where there have been changes in the employer's management the employer may have considerable evidential difficulties in rebutting evidence of this nature.

By Statute, Statutory Instrument and EEC Directive

4.14   Variation can take place by statute—the Equal Pay Act 1970 and the right to return to work after pregnancy are but two examples. The Protection of Employment (Transfer of Undertakings) Regulations 1981 are an example of a statutory instrument effecting variations. It will be necessary to keep a sharp eye on Europe to see what variations may come from that source.

Unilateral Variation

4.15   In the absence either of a contractual right to vary or the employee's consent, the employer may nevertheless when faced with the circumstances where it is necessary for him to do so, impose changes on his workforce. However, it is beyond doubt that in the absence of a contractual right, express or implied, or the employee's consent, again express or implied the employer cannot substantially vary the terms of the existing contract, and such change must be imposed by means of dismissal and subsequent re-engagement on the varied terms.

Dismissal and Re-engagement

4.16   De facto variation can be brought about by the employer terminating the existing contract and offering to re-engage the employees on varied terms. While such action would undoubtedly constitute a dismissal for the purposes of EPCA, in appropriate circumstances, an employer will be able to show that those dismissals were not unfair. In *Hollister* v. *National Farmers Union*[11] Mr. Hollister was employed as one of the N.F.U.'s group secretaries in Cornwall. When the employers decided on a reorganisation involving a change in the financial arrangements Hollister objected on grounds that there had been no consultation about the changes and that the financial provisions were inadequate. He refused to sign a new contract and was dismissed. On his subsequent unfair dismissal claim the tribunal held that the reorganisation was essential for business reasons and that there was no obligation to consult with Mr. Hollister and consequently his dismissal was fair because it was for "some other substantial reason". On his appeal to the E.A.T. his appeal was allowed. The E.A.T. held that, whilst the tribunal were correct in holding that the dismissal was for some other substantial reason, the consultation by the employers had not been sufficient to enable them to discharge the onus of showing that they had acted reasonably. The employer's subsequent appeal to the Court of Appeal was successful. The Court of Appeal observed that the need for reorganisation need not be a pressing one without which the business would come to a halt—as long as it is made for sound business reasons it will be a substantial reason for dismissal.

Imposition

In Hollister there was a clear dismissal by the employer. In other **4.17** similar cases the dismissal has come about by virtue of the employee resigning and claiming constructive dismissal. However, in circumstances where the employer seeks to impose a change to the employee's terms of employment, the employee is not confined to resigning and claiming constructive dismissal and indeed if the variation sought to be imposed was of a relatively minor nature, he may not be entitled to do so. His alternative course of action is to continue working refusing to accept the breach and suing for damages. This was the course of action taken by the employees in both *Burdett-Coutts and Others* v. *Hertfordshire County Council*[12] and *Rigby* v. *Ferodo Ltd.*[13]

---

[11] [1979] I.C.R. 542.
[12] [1984] I.R.L.R. 91.
[13] [1988] I.C.R. 29.

VARIATION

In the first of these cases the County Council sent a letter to their school dinner ladies headed "amendment of contract of service—general kitchen assistants". The letter set out various detailed amendments which operated so as to reduce the pay of the dinner ladies. The letter continued "this letter is a formal notice of these changes in your contract of service. . . . I hope you will continue in the school meals service". The ladies stayed in their posts and received reduced wages but brought a High Court action for the recovery of arrears of wages and for a declaration that the Council were not entitled to vary their employment contracts unilaterally. Their action succeeded, the High Court holding that the Council was not entitled to vary the terms of the contract of employment unilaterally and their attempt amounted to a repudiation. However the court went on to hold that whilst the employees could have accepted this repudiation and resigned they were equally entitled to stand on the original contract and claim their contractual rights under it. The employers sought to argue that because the notice given of the changes in the contractual terms was at least as long as that required to terminate the ladies' contract of employment, the letter should be construed as a notice of termination and offer of re-employment on new terms. The High Court rejected this construction the letter did not put the matter like that at all.

Similarly in *Rigby* v. *Ferodo Ltd.* (see above), it was held by The House of Lords that a unilateral imposition of a wage cut by the employer constituted a repudiatory breach of contract entitling the employees to stand by the original contractual terms as to pay and to bring an action for damages. Their Lordships also rejected the employer's argument that their action could be construed as notice of termination of the contract and held that the employee was entitled to recover damages for breach of contract which, because the contract continued in existence, were not limited to the time at which it could first have been lawfully terminated, *i.e.* the period of notice.

It is clear from these cases that if the employer wishes to impose variations by terminating the existing contract and re-offering employment on the varied terms he must give clear notice under the existing contract.

CHAPTER 5

SUSPENSION

Introduction

Many people may consider that suspending an employee can only arise in cases where there is an allegation against an employee which needs to be investigated and for that reason the employee should not be on the premises of the employer whilst that investigation is carried out.

In fact in certain circumstances a suspension can be part of the disciplinary procedure. It may also arise in the circumstances where for medical grounds an employee must be suspended from work and there may be occasions where employees are laid off because there is, for example, insufficient work for them. This chapter deals with all three situations.

Disciplinary Procedure

Subject to the point made in paragraph 5.4 below about custom and **5.1** practice, there is no implied right for the employer to suspend an employee as a disciplinary sanction. Under section 55(2)(*c*) of E.P.C.A. 1978 to do so may justify the employee terminating the contract, with or without notice by reason of the employer's conduct. In *Western Excavating (E.C.C.) Ltd.* v. *Sharp*[1] the Court of Appeal said section

---

[1] [1978] I.C.R. 221.

SUSPENSION

55(2)(c) will normally come into play where the employer has been guilty of conduct which under the general law of contract entitles the employee to terminate the relationship if the employer's conduct is such that it is a significant breach going to the root of the contract; or which shows that the employer no longer intends to be bound by one or more of the essential terms of the contract so that the employee is entitled to treat himself as discharged from any further performance.

5.2 In such a situation, where an employer suspends an employee as a punishment under the disciplinary procedure and there is no express right to do so, the employer is at risk of a claim being brought.

5.3 If the employee takes no action but returns to work after the suspension and has not been paid during that suspension there may be a claim for arrears of salary during the period of suspension. In the case of *Hanley* v. *Pease & Partners Ltd.*[2] it was held that where the employers had suspended the employee for a day the employee's claim is technically one for damages for refusing to allow him to perform his contract of service. This, however, might not be how the claim would now be put.

5.4 It is important for the employer specifically to reserve in the contract of employment the right to suspend an employee with or without pay. However, in *Marshall* v. *English Electric Company Ltd.*[3] and *Bird* v. *British Celanese Ltd.*[4] it was held that the right to suspend an employee could be implied by custom or practice. Whilst this may be the position it is nevertheless dangerous for the employer to rely upon this principle. The law has moved on considerably since those cases and the tribunals may well expect an employer to take a more enlightened approach to this issue.

5.5 It was stated by Lord Goddard in *Marshall* v. *English Electric Company Ltd.*[5] (see above) that

> "what is called suspension is in truth dismissal with an intimation at the end of so many days, or it may be hours, the man will be re-employed if he chooses to apply for re-instatement."

That may have been the position at common law then but it is not so now. Note also that *Marshall* was not a unanimous decision and the decision of Du Parcq L.J. (the dissenting view) may carry more weight now.

---

[2] [1915] 1 K.B. 698.
[3] [1945] 1 All E.R. 653.
[4] [1945] 1 All E.R. 488.
[5] At p. 655.

5.6 The A.C.A.S. Code of Practice at paragraph 12(c) makes it clear that suspension as a disciplinary sanction is only permitted if it is allowed for by an express or implied condition of the contract of employment.

5.7 At paragraph 11 of the Code there is also reference to suspension while the case is investigated but it makes it clear that such suspension, whilst it does not need to be contractual, should be with pay. Again this is an area where it is strongly recommended that in any statement dealing with the disciplinary procedure the employer should set out what happens in the event of the need to investigate an allegation against an employee.

5.8 One important drafting point which needs to be borne in mind relates to the suspension of an employee pending the hearing of an appeal against dismissal. In *Savage* v. *J. Sainsbury Ltd.*[6] the company's disciplinary procedure provided for an employee to be "suspended" without pay where an appeal against a decision to dismiss was taken up. If the appeal did not succeed then the dismissal stood but if the employee was reinstated then he would receive his salary for the period of his suspension without pay.

5.9 It is important because it has relevance as to the time within which an employee can make a claim in the industrial tribunal. If the dismissal only takes effect at the date the appeal is heard and is unsuccessful then the employee may have vital extra days in which to lodge the application. Consequently if the employer wishes to have a similar provision to that which Sainsburys included in the disciplinary procedure it may be sensible for the disciplinary procedure to go on to say that in the event of the appeal being unsuccessful termination of employment takes effect on the date the employee was originally dismissed.

Suspension on Medical Grounds

5.10 Under section 19 of E.P.C.A. 1978 an employee may be entitled to remuneration from his employer while he is suspended for a period not exceeding 26 weeks as a result of any statutory requirement or subordinate legislation or any recommendation in any provisional code of practice issued or approved under section 16 of the Health & Safety at Work Act 1974. A list can be found in Schedule 1 to E.P.C.A. but it is limited.

5.11 There are excluded categories: those who are employed overseas, dock workers, short term employees (that is, those on a fixed term contract for three months or less) or those who are casual employees.

---

[6] [1980] I.R.L.R. 109.

SUSPENSION

5.12 In order to qualify for the payment the employee must have completed one month's continuous employment ending with the day upon which the suspension begins. It should be noted that an employee is treated as suspended from his work if he continues to be employed by his employer but is not provided with work or does not perform the work he normally performed before the suspension. Having said that, under section 24 of E.P.C.A. if the employee refuses suitable alternative work whether or not it is work under his contract of employment, or, if he does not comply with a reasonable requirement imposed by the employer with a view to ensuring that his services are available, then the right to any payment may be lost.

5.13 If the employer dismisses the employee rather than suspending him then the employee may have a right to bring a claim in the industrial tribunal after only one month of continuous employment (section 64(2) of E.P.C.A.). The employee does have to bring the claim however within three months of dismissal.

5.14 As with statutory sick pay there is nothing to stop the employer increasing an employee's rights but it is probable that such a right will be linked to an occupational sick pay scheme.

Lay off and Guarantee Payments

5.15 Under section 12 of E.P.C.A. an employee is entitled to certain guarantee payments ("G.P.") in the event of there being no work for the employee in accordance with the contract of employment. It must be stressed, however, that these rights do not entitle the employer to lay off employees. This right depends solely upon what is contained in the contract of employment which may also govern matters such as the level of the guarantee payment.

5.16 It is important to distinguish between a lay off for redundancy purposes and a lay off which gives rise to a guarantee payment. To start with a G.P. will arise where there is a diminution in the employer's requirement for work rather than for the number of employees to do the work. Sections 81 and 87–89 of E.P.C.A. deal with a lay off which amounts to a redundancy. However, it must be borne in mind that if the lay off is for long enough, normally four weeks, then the employee may be entitled to a redundancy payment. Even if the employee has received a G.P. this does not preclude him from seeking a redundancy payment once those conditions have been fulfilled.

5.17 Under section 12, where an employee throughout a day during any part of which he would normally be required to work in accordance with his contract of employment, is not provided with work by his employer by reason of:

(a) a diminution in the requirements of the employer's business for work of the kind which the employee is employed to do; or

(b) any other occurrence affecting the normal working week of the employer's business in relation to work of the kind which the employee is employed to do.

then he may be entitled to a G.P.

5.18 Section 13 deals with the excluded classes of employees in relation to G.P.s and include, *inter alia*, those employed under a contract for a fixed term of three months or less, casual employees or where there is a collective contracting out which is dealt with below.

5.19 Under section 12 it is therefore necessary to identify what is a day an employee would "normally be required to work." A day means a day ending at midnight; if shift work covers two days, one day may count. In one case employers kept their factory open on a limited basis during the annual shut down and were held not to be liable to pay G.P.s on days during that period when there was no work available as employees were not normally required to work at that time.

5.20 When assessing when the work is normally done, if the employee is part time, then the entitlement to payments only arise for those days when the employee actually works part time; not for the period when work is not available but which days the employee would not normally work. In the case of a part time employee, that is one who is working between eight and 16 hours, the right to a G.P. only arises if they have completed five years continuous employment, providing, however, that the employee is working more than 16 hours when the right to a G.P. arises and such employee has one month's continuous employment.

5.21 The second limb of section 12 is where there is an occurrence affecting the business. Normally the occurrence has to be an external factor rather than a voluntary one as in *North* v. *Pavleigh Ltd.*[7] where it was held not to be an occurrence because no work was available on account of the Jewish religious holiday, and the employer did not normally close for these holidays.

5.22 The calculation is dealt with under section 14 by multiplying the number of normal working hours in the relevant day by the guaranteed hourly rate. The calculation could be complex but as there is a current maximum daily rate of £11.85 (reviewable annually by the Secretary of State for Employment) the calculation should be relatively straight forward.

5.23 The maximum an employee can be paid is for five days in any three month period. Furthermore under section 16 of E.P.C.A. where there is a

---

[7] [1977] I.R.L.R. 461.

contractual right to a guaranteed minimum payment that payment can be set off against a statutory liability and likewise the statutory G.P. can be set off against the contractual payment. In *Cartright* v. *G. Clancey Ltd.*[8] the E.A.T. affirmed that the contractual payments were to be taken into account when calculating whether G.P.s had been paid for up to five days during a three month period. Therefore it is not possible to obtain a further five day's payment during the three month period by relying on the statutory right to a G.P. although there have been five contractual G.P.s.

5.24 Even though all the conditions are fulfilled for making a G.P. it is still possible for the right to the payment to be lost. Under section 13(3) of E.P.C.A., where there is a strike, lock out or other industrial action involving any employee of the employer or of an associated employer no G.P. is payable. Note, however, the case of *Peplow* v. *Bennett Swift Lines (Birmingham) Ltd.*[9] where work was suspended because the customer of the employer had a strike on his premises which affected the employer and led to the tribunal deciding that this amounted to "an occurrence."

5.25 An employee may also lose the right to a G.P. if the employer has offered suitable alternative work. Although the terminology is not dissimilar to that under section 82 of E.P.C.A., different considerations apply. The period of the lay off is usually much shorter than in a redundancy situation and the tribunal is likely to take a more restrictive approach of the employee's duties. For example in *Roberts and Howells* v. *Firth Cleveland Engineering Ltd.*[10] an employee refused to do a job involving shovelling because he was a skilled man. The tribunal was unsympathetic. Had there been some medical reason why he could not have done the work then the tribunal said it may have taken a different approach. (See also Chap. 4, para. 4.5 on "variation").

5.26 The employer may also impose reasonable requirements which if not complied with could also disentitle the employee to a G.P. For example in *Bufton* v. *Hall & Son*[11] employees were sent home and told to come back the following day because there was no heating oil but because the following day they held a meeting and decided not to return to work their claim was dismissed because they had not complied with the reasonable requirements of the employer.

---

[8] [1983] I.R.L.R. 355.
[9] Unreported: 1982 C.O.I.T. 1324/30.
[10] C.O.I.T. 1774/33.
[11] C.O.I.T. 905/27.

The Contractual Position

Unusually, it is possible to contract out of these provisions. However it **5.27** cannot merely be done by agreement for example between union and management that employees would not present G.P. claims because that would be in breach of section 140(1) of E.P.C.A. In order for the agreement to be effective all the parties must make an application to the appropriate minister for an order to be made under section 18 of E.P.C.A. even if the alternative agreement is not as favourable as the statutory provisions.

As can be seen from the above there is some scope for the employer **5.28** protecting himself by contract. The most important protection is obviously the express right to suspend the contract of employment (with pay) rather than terminate it. As said above, notwithstanding the cases of *Bird* and *Marshall* (see above) there must be a term in the contract before the employer can suspend it for there is no implied right to suspend the contract.[12] There is some academic debate that if there is a contractual right to lay off an employee indefinitely, then there is no implied term that such a lay off can be for a reasonable time only[13] although section 88 of E.P.C.A. may still come into play as that is a statutory right which cannot be excluded.

Whatever the position it is important that an employer seeks to avoid **5.29** any claim, for example, for constructive dismissal by reserving the right to suspend the contract in the contract itself.

It is not every employer who will want to include contractual terms **5.30** dealing with G.P.s. Nor indeed will every employer regard suspension as an acceptable disciplinary sanction. Nevertheless, an employer may wish to make it clear that he is entitled to suspend an employee while investigating any allegation and that an employee unless re-instated on appeal is dismissed from the date he was first told his employment was being terminated.

---

[12] See *Neads* v. *C.A.V. Ltd.* [1983] I.R.L.R. 360.
[13] See *Kenneth Macrae & Co. Ltd.* v. *Dawson* [1984] I.R.L.R. 5.

Chapter 6

TERMINATION

Introduction

There are a variety of methods by which parties to a contract of **6.1**
employment may choose to end that relationship. It may be mutual or it
may be unilateral action by one or other party. In general consensual
termination is acceptable unless one party (usually the employee)
alleges pressure to give their consent. However, with unilateral termination of the contract of employment the question arises whether the party
alleging entitlement to terminate the contract was in fact able to do so.
The position is complicated by the dual systems which exist side by
side, both of which need to be considered. At common law either party
may be able to allege breach of contract against the other. By statute
an employee may be able to bring a claim based on his statutory rights
not to be unfairly dismissed.

It is important to note that some areas, such as resignation by the **6.2**
employee, may straddle the divide between consensual and unilateral
termination. For example the employee may feel that he has no choice
but to offer his resignation. Such cases will be dealt with by unilateral
termination, because in truth there is no agreement to terminate.
Furthermore it is necessary to note that some acts by an employer
which might not normally be thought of as constituting a unilateral
termination (or dismissal) (*e.g.* non-renewal of a fixed term contract) are,
under statute, deemed to be a dismissal.

Termination by Agreement

6.3   The parties are free to agree to terminate the contract between them at any time. Just as there is no obligation for a contract of employment to be in writing, or in any particular form there is no obligation for a termination of a contract to be recorded in any particular way. It should be noted that there is a statutory right to written reasons for dismissal where the employee alleges he has been dismissed (*i.e.* he has not consented to leave the employment).[1]

6.4   The Courts have had a difficult task in the area of consensual agreements because, if there has been no dismissal, an employee will find that he has no claim against his employer. The Courts therefore have to distinguish between genuine agreement and the case where the employee has been pressured into accepting the agreement and later wishes to bring a claim against his employer. Thus, for example, in *Statford* v. *Donovan*[2] the E.A.T. held that the employer and employee had reached a genuine agreement on the terms upon which the employee would leave employment. Often the tribunals have been faced with a situation equivalent to "leave or be dismissed" but there had been no such threat here. The E.A.T. stated that the mere fact that the agreement was reached against a background of disciplinary proceedings being taken against the employee did not render the consensual termination a dismissal. It was rightly pointed out that in such circumstances an employee can nonetheless go to Court following an agreement which had been genuinely reached between himself and the employer. See also *Crowley* v. *Ashland*[3] where an employer suggested that an employee might resign on terms agreeable to both sides and that court held this did not mean that the employee had been dismissed.

6.5   In *Glencross* v. *Dymoke*[4] the employee was offered the alternatives of redundancy or an agreement covering the use by the employee of the company premises, on his own account. The E.A.T. said

> "if one looks at the reality of the situation it is plain . . . that the employee was being told that his job was going to come to an end."

Accordingly this was a case of "leave or else."

---

[1] See E.P.C.A. 1978 s.53.
[2] [1981] I.R.L.R. 108.
[3] Unreported: E.A.T. 31/79.
[4] [1979] I.R.L.R. 536.

One option that used to be favoured by employers was that an **6.6** employee would be asked to agree that particular conduct by him/her would automatically terminate the contract of employment. The employers would then argue that he had not terminated the contract by dismissal, but that the contract had terminated by agreement. This was disposed of in *Johnson Mathey* v. *Igbo*[5] where the Court of Appeal held that such a scheme fell foul of E.P.C.A. s.140. This section prevents (in almost all circumstances) an employee from contracting out of his statutory right to sue in respect of an alleged unfair dismissal. The case concerned an applicant who wished to take extended leave from work. She signed an agreement in which she agreed that if she did not report for work on a particular date her employment would terminate automatically. The Court pointed out that if this was permissible then an employer could choose to cover any particular misdemeanour and allege that the contract had terminated automatically. As the Court of Appeal pointed out this would turn an otherwise unconditional right not to be unfairly dismissed into a conditional right.

Resignation

Resignation, unlike termination by agreement, does not automatically **6.7** preclude an employee from bringing a claim for unfair dismissal against his employers. By virtue of E.P.C.A. s.55 (which contains a definition of dismissal for unfair dismissal purposes) dismissal includes resignations in situations where the employee was entitled to resign because of the employer's conduct. There is no reference to consensual termination in section 55. It is clear that "resign or be dismissed" is a constructive dismissal by the employer if the employee resigns (*c.f. East Sussex* v. *Walker*.[6] The dismissal may of course be fair.

In *Hart* v. *British Veterinary Association*[7] the E.A.T. said that the **6.8** industrial tribunal should look at the circumstances surrounding any termination and if the employer had made a suggestion to the employee the correct course would be for industrial tribunals to look at the words

---

[5] [1986] I.R.L.R. 215.
[6] [1972] I.T.R. 280.
[7] Unreported: E.A.T. 145/678.

to see whether they were clear. If they were not then the industrial tribunal should look and see if the surrounding circumstances shed light on their meaning.

6.9   In *Morton Sundour Fabrics* v. *Shaw*[8] the employer told Shaw that his employment would be coming to an end and that he would be made redundant. However the employer did not say when this event would occur. The High Court said

> "as a matter of law an employer cannot dismiss his employee by saying 'I intend to dispense with your services at some time in the coming months'. In order to terminate the contract of employment the notice must either specify the date or contain material from which that date is positively ascertainable."

This case was prior to the Industrial Relations Act 1971 and was deciding whether, at common law, the employer had terminated the contract. Note, however, that it might be that if an employer intimates to his employee that he will be dismissed then the employer would be in breach of the implied terms of mutual trust and confidence. In *Devon County* v. *Cook*[9] although on the facts of the case the warning given to the employee did not amount to constructive dismissal, the Court said

> "the case put on this man's behalf amounts to the proposition that once there is a forecasted redundancy and a man of his own volition goes off and gets another job he is automatically entitled to say that the employer's conduct forced him to go. Of course, this cannot be right. It may be the true position or it may not according to the circumstances and the relevant conduct of both parties."

6.10   On the other hand in *East Sussex* v. *Walker*[10] the applicant was told that her job was going to end and she was expressly asked to resign. It was held that she had been dismissed by reason of redundancy.

6.11   An employer should, however, be free to and indeed should warn his employees of impending redundancy. E.P.C.A. s. 99 requires an employer to consult with independent recognised trade unions in respect of redundancies in some cases. Clearly parliament could not have intended that by carrying out his obligations to consult he was constructively dismissing the employees concerned.

---

[8] [1967] I.T.R. 84.
[9] [1977] I.R.L.R. 188.
[10] [1972] I.T.R. 280.

It is sometimes necessary to determine the meaning of the words **6.12** used. The corollary to the *Morton Sundour* case is that if an employee states that he is going to resign at some unspecified future time then this is not resignation. The tribunals treat the question as one of fact.[11] The cases on resignation show that tribunals consider first whether the words were ambiguous or not. The same principle applies to verbal dismissals. If the words are not ambiguous then provided the employer (or the person to whom they spoke) understood them as such the tribunal will not inquire.[12] However the Courts appear to demand a high standard of proof before they will accept that the words are unambiguous or that they should not look at the surrounding circumstances (compare for example *Stern* v. *Simpson*[13] and *Sovereign House* v. *Savage*.)[14] If the words are ambigious then the Court will ask what a reasonable employer would have meant the words to mean, *e.g. Tanner* v. *Kean*.[15] In this case the employer told the employee "you're finished". This was held not to be a dismissal having regard to the surrounding circumstances and the subsequent events.

Words said in the heat of the moment may, if retracted sufficiently **6.13** quickly, be nullified. In *Martin* v. *Yeoman Aggregates*,[16] five minutes after having unequivocally dismissed the employee the employer withdrew the words and full disciplinary proceedings were substituted. E.A.T. held that the employee had not been dismissed.

Project Work

This is a relatively rare reason for termination of a contract but the **6.14** possibilities have been recognised, and the Courts have held that termination by virtue of completion of a project is not equivalent to a "dismissal." Thus in *Wiltshire County Council* v. *NATFHE*[17] the Court of Appeal said[18]

---

[11] See *Martin* v. *Glynwed* [1983] I.R.L.R. 198.
[12] See *Southern* v. *Franks Charsley* [1981] I.R.L.R. 278, C.A. and *Gayle* v. *Gilbert* [1978] I.C.R. 1149.
[13] [1983] I.R.L.R. 52.
[14] [1989] I.R.L.R. 115.
[15] [1978] I.R.L.R. 110.
[16] [1983] I.C.R. 314.
[17] [1980] I.C.R. 455.
[18] *Per* Denning M.R. at p. 460.

"if there is a contract by which a man is to do a particular task or to carry out a particular purpose then when that task or purpose comes to an end the contract is discharged by performance."

A contract for a particular purpose which is fulfilled is discharged by performance and does not amount to a dismissal. Examples were given of seamen recruited for a voyage or a contract for the duration of the life of the present sovereign. The test is whether the term of the contract is indeterminate of ascertainment.

Death of Employer

6.15   Death of an individual employer terminates any contract pursuant to which he employed anyone.

Insolvency of Employer

6.16   Contrast receivership which does not terminate employment contracts and voluntary/compulsory liquidation and the position in relation to an administrator.

Frustration

6.17   The common law principles of frustration of contracts apply to contracts of employment. The common law judges felt that if circumstances altered after the contract had been entered into so that one or other of the parties could legitimately say "It was not this that I contracted to do" then he ought to be released from his side of the bargain and not be penalised for failing to complete what he had undertaken to do.

6.18   Frustration of contracts of employment arises in two main areas—sickness and imprisonment.

Sickness

The Courts have held on several occasions that an employee's **6.19** sickness may frustrate a contract of employment. Whether it will do so will depend upon the circumstances of the particular case. In *Marshall v. Harland & Wolff*,[19] the basic question was "was the employee's incapacity looked at before the purported dismissal of such a nature or did it appear likely to continue for such a period that further performance of his obligations in the future would either be impossible or would be a thing radically different from that undertaken by him and agreed to be accepted by the employer under the agreed terms of his employment."[20] The relevant facts identified in this particular case were:

(a) under the terms of the contract whether any provision for sickness payment had been made. Obviously if sick pay was still being paid an employer would find it exceedingly difficult to argue that the contract had been frustrated;

(b) how long the employment was likely to last in the absence of sickness;

(c) the nature of the employment;

(d) the nature and length of the illness;

(e) the period of present employment—the longer the employment relationship the greater the sickness required to frustrate.

A further relevant factor has been whether the job can reasonably be **6.20** expected to be kept open any longer.[21] It will of course be relevant that even if there has been a dismissal the employer will be able to argue that such a dismissal is fair.

There is no requirement for an employer to indicate when he accepts **6.21** the contract is frustrated. In *Hart* v. *Marshall*[22] the fact that the employer went on accepting sick notes from the employee (without paying him and after having engaged a replacement) did not prevent the contract from being frustrated.

---

[19] [1972] I.C.R. 101.
[20] *Per* Sir John Donaldson at p. 105.
[21] *Eggstores* v. *Leibovici* [1977] I.C.R. 260; see Chap. 6 para. 6.22 below.
[22] [1977] I.R.L.R. 51.

TERMINATION

6.22 The Courts naturally feel less reluctant to allow frustration of long fixed term contracts, as opposed to periodic contracts. In *Eggstores* v. *Leibovici* (see above) it was accepted that periodic contracts could be frustrated (the alternative being for an employer being to dismiss the employee). Two examples were put forward. One possibility was a sudden crippling illness of the employee which would obviously preclude the employee from working subsequently. Secondly, with a long standing illness, after which there will come a time at which the contract will be frustrated. Thus, in *Hart* v. *Marshall* (see above) the 20 months absence of a key worker frustrated the contract.

6.23 Although in an earlier E.A.T. decision[23] it was stated that periodic contracts could not be frustrated, and the Courts would examine the fairness of the dismissal, the Court of Appeal in *Notcutt* v. *Universal Equipment*[24] stated that in principle there was no objection to a periodic contract being frustrated. It will, it is suggested, remain easier to show that a fixed term contract has been frustrated. Furthermore, normally the tribunals will wish to consider the merits of the matter, rather than allowing the employer to rely on frustration.

6.24 Note that an employer may not have to wait until the contract is frustrated before he is able to dismiss an employee fairly.

Imprisonment

6.25 This has been a more problematic area for the Courts. Frustration normally applies when neither party is at fault, otherwise the termination would be by way of repudiation or breach. (Compare this with, in a non-employment context, *Maritime National Fish Ltd.* v. *The Ocean Trawlers Ltd.*)[25] The Courts have struggled to decide whether the criminal activities of an employee, which lead to imprisonment can be characterised as repudiatory conduct or as being conduct resulting in frustration.

6.26 The most recent decision, at Court of Appeal level was *F. C. Sheppard* v. *Jerome*[26] which accepted that a borstal sentence of

---

[23] *Harman* v. *Flexible Lamp* [1980] I.R.L.R. 418.
[24] [1986] I.R.L.R. 216.
[25] [1935] A.C. 524.
[26] [1986] 3 All E.R. 589.

between six months and two years was capable of frustrating the contract. The Court held that the employee could not rely on his own default to counter the argument that the contract had been frustrated. The employee had argued (relying on *L.T.E.* v. *Clarke*)[27] that he had repudiated the contract and this repudiation had been accepted by the employer. Therefore he had been dismissed. It will be noted that if the employee had claimed wrongful dismissal then it would not have availed him to assert that he had repudiated the contract. The employers could then simply argue that they were accepting his repudiation.[28] There have been cases where a prison sentence did not frustrate the contract. In the case of *Mecca Ltd.* v. *Sheppherd*[29] a 24 day sentence of which the employee served 20 days was held not to frustrate the contract. It was pointed out that the employer did not at the time consider that the contract was frustrated nor was the absence longer than some summer holidays.

In *Harrington* v. *Kent C.C.*[30] the employee lodged an appeal following **6.27** his conviction. However following his conviction his employer had written to him stating that the contract had been terminated since the employee could not continue to perform his side of the contract. This was upheld by the E.A.T..

An employer may dismiss for unproven criminal activity (gross mis- **6.28** conduct for example) before a trial provided he honestly believes on reasonable grounds in the guilt of the employee. The most widely known case is *B.H.S.* v. *Burchell*[31] and it is very often quoted in tribunals. The subsequent acquittal of the employee does not render any dismissal automatically unfair.[32] There is no legal obligation on an employer to wait for the outcome of the criminal proceedings.[33]

It may not matter whether the contract is or is not frustrated because **6.29** in most cases the employer will mark the end of the relationship by telling the employee it is at an end thereby probably creating a dismissal. If there is a genuine frustration employers should therefore be careful as to what they do administratively.

---

[27] [1981] I.R.L.R. 166.
[28] *Boston Deep Sea* v. *Ansell* [1988] 39 Ch.D. 339.
[29] Unreported: E.A.T. 379/78.
[30] [1980] I.R.L.R. 353.
[31] [1978] I.R.L.R. 379.
[32] *Da Costa* v. *Optolis* [1976] I.R.L.R. 178.
[33] *Conway* v. *Mathew Wright & Neck* [1977] I.R.L.R. 80.

Unilateral Termination

Termination By Employer Without Notice

6.30   An employer has the ability in certain circumstances to dismiss an employee summarily (without notice). This right was left unaffected by the statutory framework of minimum notice periods.[34] Of course an employee with the necessary statutory qualifications may always bring a claim for unfair dismissal. Summary dismissal will only be justified in cases where the employee's conduct has been particularly grave.

Possible Actions for Summary Dismissal

6.31   It is necessary to appreciate that a summary dismissal may be challenged in two entirely different actions, wrongful dismissal through the Courts or unfair dismissal through the tribunals. There are other related options such as injunctions or public law remedies. The wrongful dismissal option is only applicable where an employer has "breached" one of the terms of the contract, *i.e.* dismissed without due notice under the contract. The employer may claim in his defence that the employee was in prior breach of the contract himself and that by summary dismissal he was merely accepting the employee's breach. The remedies are dealt with in more detail at paragraph 6.38 *et seq* and 6.68 *et seq.*

Action Which Justifies Summary Dismissal

6.32   Thus it is not surprising that at common law the Judges have decided that before an employer can dismiss an employee summarily he must

---

[34] E.P.C.A. 1978 s.49(5).

be guilty of conduct which is conduct indicative that he no longer feels bound by the contract (in other words the employee commits a repudiation of the contract or a fundamental breach of the contract, *e.g. Laws* v. *London Chronicle*).[35]

Before citing some examples, two points should be noted. First, in **6.33** *Wilson* v. *Racher*[36] it was pointed out that each case turned on its own facts.[37] Second, although an employee owes his employer a general duty of "obedience" social circumstances have changed.

> "What would in the context of the duty of obedience today be regarded as almost an attitude of Czar-serf which is to be found in some of the older cases where a dismissed employee failed to recover damages would, I venture to think, be decided differently today."[38]

This case concerned an employee who used insulting and abusive language to his employer following his employer's comments to him about (in the Court's opinion) trifling matters. For an act of misconduct such as this (*i.e.* a one-off) it has to be determined whether this was deliberate flouting of the essential terms of the contract, which was incompatible with the continued contract of employment. In the context the remarks did not merit summary dismissal. In *Jupiter General* v. *Schroff* (see above) the employee deliberately recommended the issue of an insurance policy knowing that his managing governor had refused to issue it a few days earlier. This was held to warrant summary dismissal. In *Pepper* v. *Webb*[39] the gardener, whose work had deteriorated and who had become insolent was rude to his employer who summarily dismissed him. This was upheld by the Court of Appeal. In the *Wilson* v. *Racher* case referred to above, five years later the Court pointed out that the gardener's attitude in the earlier case had been the last straw whereas in the *Wilson* v. *Racher* case there had been no such history of difficulties. In *Jupiter General* v. *Schroff* the Privy Council said that there would have to be "exceptional circumstances" before an employer could dismiss for a one-off offence.

Two examples of deliberate conduct which may lead to a justifiable **6.34** summary dismissal are, first, dishonesty, (see *Boston* v. *Ansell*[40] where the act in question was the acceptance of a secret commission, and

---

[35] [1959] 1 W.L.R. 698.
[36] [1974] I.C.R. 428.
[37] Note also The Privy Council case of *Jupiter General* v. *Schroff* [1937] 3 All E.R. 67 below.
[38] *per* Lord Edmund Davies at p. 430 in *Wilson* v. *Racher*, see above.
[39] [1969] 1 W.L.R. 514.
[40] [1888] 39 Ch.D 339.

the company was held to have a defence to a wrongful dismissal action despite the fact that it was a one-off incident by the employee) and secondly, industrial action, since it is usually a deliberate breach of the terms of the contract.

6.35   It is open to an employer when contracting with the employee to point out to him that that particular conduct will be viewed very seriously. Similarly with work rules, it is open to the employer to specify the seriousness of the breach. This will aid the employer in both unfair and wrongful dismissal cases, but care should be taken not to limit in the contract what will be taken as gross misconduct justifying summary dismissal.

It is suggested that involuntary conduct is less likely to lead to justifiable summary dismissal.

6.36   When dealing with accidental conduct the Courts will look at the results of the action[41] or the potential consequences.[42] In the latter case an airline pilot landed his plane sufficiently poorly to cause concern to the crew and passengers. Bearing in mind the potential consequences should he repeat his poor performance the company was held to be justified in summarily dismissing him. This was an extreme case, where not only was the employer entitled to dismiss the employee for neglect, he was also entitled to dismiss for neglect on a one-off basis.

Consequences of an Unjustified Summary Dismissal

6.37   The standard response to a contested summary dismissal will be to lodge a claim for wrongful or unfair dismissal (see below for the relationship between the two). Which will be the most advantageous in each case will depend partly on the length of notice period the employee is entitled to. The highly paid employee entitled to six months notice may well find it advantageous to sue for wrongful dismissal. This is because of the statutory maximum awarded in unfair dismissal awards (and the infrequent use by tribunals of their ability to order reinstatement or re-engagement). On the other hand, the relative speed of unfair dismissal proceedings may justify those being brought first, albeit a High Court writ may also be issued simultaneously.

---

[41] *Savage* v. *British India* [1930] 46 T.L.R. 294.
[42] *Taylor* v. *Alidair* [1978] I.R.L.R. 82.

Establishing the Period of Notice

The first matter is therefore to establish the notice entitlement of the **6.38**
employee in question. There is a statutory minimum (save where
summary dismissal is justified). Thus an employee who has worked for
one month or more for the employer in question is entitled to one week's
notice. After two years he is entitled to a further week's notice.
Thereafter with each extra year's work he is entitled to an extra week's
notice up to a maximum of 12 weeks.[43]

However, this is a statutory minimum and the parties usually provide
by contract what the notice period will be. If the contract is silent then
the employee will be entitled to reasonable notice. This will vary with the
seniority and length of service of the employee in question. In *Hill* v.
Parsons[44] the Court of Appeal decided that one month was far "too
short" for a 63 year old professional man with 35 years of service. For
company directors the norm is now probably one year and, as indicated, note the Companies Act 1985's overall limitation to five years for
directors of public companies.

Wrongful Dismissal

The action is a basic common law action for damages for breach of **6.39**
contract. The employee will issue proceedings in the County Court or
High Court depending on the value of the claim. An action may be
brought in the County Court provided the amount claimed does not
exceed £5,000.[45] An injured party is entitled to be put in the position he
could have been in if the contract had been properly performed. For
employees with, say, a three month notice in the contract damages will
be limited by the fact that the employer could have terminated the
contract lawfully, (*i.e.* in accordance with the contract) by giving three
months notice.

---

[43] E.P.C.A. 1978 s.49.
[44] [1971] 3 All E.R. 1345.
[45] County Court Act 1984 s.15(1).

What Can Dismissed Employee Claim For?

6.40   Therefore the Courts accept the argument that damages paid to the employee should be restricted by the length of the notice period. Again for contracts with no notice period the Courts will limit the damages to remuneration for a reasonable period which may be limited to the statutory minimum, although this is subject to argument in Court. Those with fixed term contracts will receive damages for the remaining period of the contract.

Thus the employee can claim as damages sums to which he would have become contractually entitled during the notice period. In *Lavarack* v. *Woods*[46] the employee was dismissed summarily (and wrongfully). He was entitled to a five year contract. He had a fixed salary on top of which he received discretionary bonuses. After he had been dismissed (but during the five year period) the employers increased the basic salary but terminated the discretionary bonuses. The employee could not claim the higher basic sums he would have earned. Nor could he claim damages in respect of the bonuses since these were discretionary. In other words the measure of damages was assessed at the date of termination in accordance with contractual liabilities at that date. What he might in practice have earned is irrelevant.

6.41   The question is therefore what would the employee be entitled to during the notice period. This obviously covers salary and other contractual benefits (perks) such as luncheon vouchers, *etc.* Company cars will also be included (although the value of the benefit for a limited period may be slight).

The Courts have also allowed employees to claim for a sum for lost training/diminution of future prospects, *Dunk* v. *George Waller.*[47]

6.42   Pensions and share option losses are complex areas which need to be considered in each case. Prima facie pension loss is limited to any loss incurred for the period of notice which should have been provided. Contrast, however, pension loss in unfair dismissal claims where the loss is assessed by applying Government Actuary principles. In *Tradewinds Airways Ltd.* v. *Fletcher,*[48] the Tribunal had taken expert ad hoc guidance instead and, on appeal, the E.A.T. held that, where the assessment of pension loss differs dramatically from the results of applying Government Actuary principles, it may be held to be erroneous and remitted for reconsideration.

---

[46] [1967] 1 Q.B. 278.
[47] [1976] I.C.R. 138.
[48] [1981] I.R.L.R. 272.

In regard to share options, the prudent employer should incorporate in contracts of employment of those eligible for a scheme, a provision making it clear that on termination no damages will be payable in respect of any share option losses. A similar provision should be put in the scheme. If the right to participate in the scheme is a term of the contract of employment, prima facie any damages on a summary dismissal because the rights cannot be exercised after termination or have to be exercised early (within three years of grant), will be the loss of profit or the difference between the income tax and capital gains tax. The latter may not matter now that both rates are 40 per cent. for high earners.

It is not uncommon for an employer, before an employee has worked **6.43** for two years thereby qualifying to be able to bring an unfair dismissal claim to review the employee's position. If the employer is dissatisfied, he can consider termination. Such termination can either be on notice or, if the notice period would take the employee past the two year continuous employment mark, summary.

It will be recalled that (subject to summary dismissal) an employee **6.44** who has worked for between one month and two years is entitled to one week's statutory notice. If an employer dismisses an employee within the week before the latter reaches the two years mark then the employee is entitled to add the statutory minimum to his employment. He will therefore be entitled to bring an unfair dismissal claim.[49] The employee cannot rely on any more generous contractual notice provisions.[50] However if an employee is summarily dismissed for gross misconduct, he cannot add on the statutory notice period.[51] The employer will decide whether the case merits the description of gross misconduct.[52]

However if an employee is unfairly and summarily dismissed before **6.45** the two year point (and cannot avail himself of s.55(5)) the Court may well consider allowing a sum for loss of statutory rights, in a wrongful dismissal claim.[53]

In *Addis* v. *Gramaphone Co. Ltd.*[54] the House of Lords held that an employee could not claim compensation for the manner of dismissal or the fact that the manner of dismissal may make it more difficult for the employee to get a new job. In *Bliss* v. *Southeast Thames*[55] the Court

---

[49] E.P.C.A. 1978 s.55(5).
[50] See *Fox Maintenance Ltd.* v. *Jackson* [1977] I.R.L.R. 87.
[51] *Ahmed* v. *National Car Parks Ltd.* unreported.
[52] *Lanton Leisure* v. *White & Gibson* [1987] I.R.L.R. 119.
[53] *Cort* v. *Charman* [1981] I.R.L.R. 437 and *Stapp* v. *Shaftesbury Society* [1972] I.R.L.R. 326.
[54] [1909] A.C. 488.
[55] [1985] I.R.L.R. 308, (C.A.).

went further saying that such a head of damages was not claimable even if it was within the contemplation of both parties that such dismissal would cause the emotional distress which occurred.

Both unemployment benefit and supplementary benefit are deductible from damages, if received by an employee during the notice period.[56]

One benefit which would not appear to be deductible is redundancy payment.[57]

Mitigation

6.46 An employee must make an effort to reduce his loss, caused by a wrongful dismissal (the same principle applies in unfair dismissal cases under E.P.C.A. s.74(4)). This means looking for and if possible obtaining new work of a broadly comparable nature. The salary received from the new work will be deducted from damages the employee receives. An employee is allowed to look around him to try and find suitable and reasonable alternative work but should not deliberately narrow his search or scope of acceptable work.[58]

Taxation

6.47 An employee who receives an award of damages in respect of a wrongful dismissal action will receive up to £30,000 tax free. Thereafter sums will be taxed.

For sums of less than £30,000 the Courts have said that the incidence of taxation is not sufficiently remote so that it ought to be ignored. The Courts will calculate what the employee would have earned (very generally) what tax the employee would have paid on those sums and

---

[56] *Parsons* v. *B.N.M. Laboratories* [1964] 1 Q.B. 95 and *Lincoln* v. *Hayman* [1982] 1 W.L.R. 488.

[57] See *Yorkshire Engineering* v. *Berkham* [1974] I.C.R. 77 and *Basnett* v. *J. & J. Jackson* [1976] I.C.R. 63.

[58] See *Shindler* v. *Northern Raincoat Company* [1960] 1 W.L.R. 1038.

award the net sum. The real winner of course is the employer who will retain money which otherwise would have been paid in taxes.[59]

For sums over £30,000 the Courts will deduct tax on the whole sum. Assuming the net sum exceeds £30,000 it will be necessary to *add* a sum to the damages to compensate the employee properly since he will be taxed on the damages in excess of £30,000.

For example if the Court awarded a gross figure of £70,000 on which £20,000 tax would be paid then the Court will work out how much has to be added on to the net figure of £50,000 which will (after tax) leave the employee with that £50,000. In other words a grossing-up exercise will take place.[60] See Appendix 5 for a worked example of these complex tax calculations.

Non-renewal of Fixed Term Contracts

Non-renewal of fixed term contracts does not constitute a dismissal at common law. By virtue of section 55(2) of E.P.C.A. if an employer does not renew a fixed term contract with an employee then this constitutes dismissal for unfair dismissal purposes. **6.48**

It is worth adding here that fixed term contracts are unusual in that in a fixed term contract of one year or more an employee can contract out of his right not to be unfairly dismissed.[61] This is presumably because the common law was felt to provide sufficient protection. If an employer wishes an employee to contract out of his rights to a redundancy payment then he must offer the employee a two year minimum contract. The exclusion in all cases must be in writing.

An employee can agree in writing to exclude protection for unfair dismissal following the non-renewal of his contract only if he has a fixed term contract of a year or more. The exclusion may only operate in respect of unfair dismissals. In relation to redundancies, the fixed term contract must be two years or more for the contracting out to be effective. **6.49**

It is an obvious ploy for an employer to offer a series of fixed term contracts to avoid the unfair dismissal/redundancy rights for employees. The Courts have therefore had to decide whether such attempts are valid or whether they fall foul of section 140 of E.P.C.A. 1978.

---

[59] See *Parsons* v. *B.N.M. Laboratories* (above) based on *B.T.C.* v. *Gourley* [1956] A.C. 185.
[60] *Shove* v. *Downs Surgical plc* [1984] I.C.R. 532.
[61] See E.P.C.A. 1978 s.142.

TERMINATION

6.50   In *B.B.C.* v. *Ioannou*[62] the extension of a fixed term contract contained a new clause excluding the employee's rights. It was decided by the majority of the Court of Appeal that the contract was a re-engagement, rather than a renewal, because of the new term. Therefore because the "extension" was for less than two years (the limit at the time) the exlcusion was void. Lord Denning stated that it was unnecessary to distinguish between renewal and re-engagement. In his view it was merely necessary to consider the length of the new contract. The Denning approach was followed in the E.A.T. in *Open University* v. *Triesman*[63] where the offending clause was only included with the extension of a fixed term contract. Finally the E.A.T. in *B.P. Oil* v. *Richards*[64] followed the *Open University* v. *Triesman* case. However the tribunal added that their decision was on the basis that the fixed term was genuine and not one intended to be renewed. In other words they were alive to the potential abuse of fixed term contracts.

> "Nothing in this decision should be taken as covering a case where employers purport to enter into fixed term contracts on the understanding that there will be periodical renewals of such contracts. In such a case as that there may be a real question whether it is in truth a fixed term contract at all".

6.51   The true position therefore appears to be far from clear. It is suggested that if employers do wish to grant an extension of a fixed term then it would be wisest to grant for a minimum of one year (to exclude unfair dismissal) or two years (to exclude redundancy) cases. Should a shorter renewal period be desired then it should be made clear that such an offer is a renewal.

Termination With Notice By Employer

6.52   It will be assumed throughout this section the notice given is in accordance with the provisions of the contract. If this is not the case then an action for wrongful dismissal (breach of contract) may arise.

6.53   Having said that it is common for an employer actually not to want an employee to work out his notice, either for fear that the employee will be exposed to confidential information, which he may take with him when

---

[62] [1975] I.C.R. 267.
[63] [1978] I.C.R. 524.
[64] Unreported: 1983 E.A.T. 768/82.

he leaves, or for fear of criminal damage (particularly in the computer industry). The employer may therefore wish to pay a sum of money, in lieu of notice, so that the employee does not work out his period of notice.

The common law position looks on "payment in lieu" as damages for breach of contract, which may be sufficient to extinguish the common law rights of the employee.[65] However, it is important to remember two points when making a payment in lieu. First, an employee is entitled to receive damages for all sums to which he is contractually entitled, and not merely his salary. Second, an employer can pay such sums net of tax. The employer can keep the "tax" because he does not have to account to the Revenue. This is a matter of election for the employer— he can pay gross or net. Both are deductible items to him and it depends on his generosity. Employees would have to argue that it is an implied term that they should receive payment in lieu gross through custom and practice. The point does not appear to have been considered yet and would appear unlikely to succeed.

One important fact to bear in mind is that the employer, to safeguard himself, should always in contracts of employment give himself the power to pay money in lieu of notice. There is no common law right to do so and what in effect the employer is doing is paying damages. The advantage of including such a clause is that an employee dismissed without notice but paid in lieu cannot assert that he has been wrongfully dismissed (assuming the correct pay in lieu is given). As in the *Parker Ginsberg* case (see above) this can have an important impact on any restrictive covenants contained in the contract. There are some cases which suggest that in some circumstances the employee may have the right to be provided with work whilst he is employed by the employer. The common law position in general is that "provided that I pay my cook she has no right to complain if I take my meals elsewhere."[66] However, it will be clear that if an employee has the right to be provided with work then this right will have to be considered in any award of damages. Thus, for instance, if the employee's pay is by reference to commission it has been held the employee should be given a reasonable opportunity to gain commission.[67] There would also appear to be special cases (airline pilots, for example) who may need to work regularly, to be able to stay in their profession. It would be interesting to see how far the

---

[65] *Dixon* v. *Stenor* [1973] I.R.L.R. 28 and *Parker Ginsberg Ltd.* v. *Parker* [1988] I.R.L.R. 483.
[66] See *Collier* v. *Sunday Referee Publishing Company Ltd.* [1940] 2 K.B. 647.
[67] *Turner* v. *Goldsmith* [1891–94] All E.R. 384 and *Langstone* v. *Chrysler* [1974] All E.R. 980.

courts would be prepared to extend this to, say, brokers, dealers or analysts in the City.

6.54 The disadvantage of a contractual right to make payment in lieu, is that it may cause a tax disadvantage for the employee. This is because it may lead to such payments being taxed under Schedule E (earned income) rather than being able to take advantage of the tax free £30,000 allowance. If the sum is viewed as damages rather than a contractual payment, then it will come within the £30,000 allowance under section 188 of the Income and Corporation Taxes Act 1988.

Unfair Dismissal

6.55 It has already been explained that the common law takes no account of the motives of the employer, but is merely concerned to see that the dismissal is in accordance with the contract. It was therefore felt necessary to give employees a statutory right not to be unfairly dismissed.[68]

6.56 What follows is merely an outline since this book does not purport to deal in detail with unfair dismissals but rather, contractual matters. In addition, decisions of industrial tribunals are not binding or even persuasive for other tribunals although they may be indicative of principles. Indeed the Court of Appeal has even deprecated the practice of the E.A.T. giving guidelines on what they consider good industrial practice.

Conditions for Bringing Unfair Dismissal Claim

6.57 There are various preconditions for the bringing of an unfair dismissal claim.

(a) The applicant is an employee.
(b) He was continuously employed for two years or more.
(c) He was not one of an excluded class of employees.
(d) He was dismissed.

---

[68] E.P.C.A. 1978 s.54(1).

An Employee

An employee is someone who works under a contract of employment. **6.58**
The main alternative is a contract for services. In the latter case the
worker is an independent party operating on his own account. See
Chapter 1 for an analysis of the tests applied to decide whether an
applicant is an employee or not.

Continuous Employment

An employee must be continuously employed for two years, before he **6.59**
is able to make a claim for unfair dismissal. There are complex rules
governing continuous employment, but in essence an employee must
have worked for two years, without a break in the contract occurring. If
a break does occur then the employee will have to start accumulating
his two years again.

The following weeks count towards continuous employment: **6.60**

(a) the employee works under a contract requiring him to work 16
    hours or more per week;
(b) he is employed under a contract normally involving him in 16
    hours or more work a week;
(c) for up to 26 weeks, he works for 8 hours or more having worked
    under a contract requiring him to work 16 hours;
(d) the employee works for 5 continuous years under a contract
    normally involving him in work for 8 hours or more;
(e) if a woman returns to work after maternity leave[69] then the weeks
    of her absence count in full;
(f) if there is no contract of employment, certain weeks can still
    count towards continuous employment;
    (i) illness up to 26 weeks will count,
    (ii) temporary cessation of work (this included an absence of
         two years in *Bentley Engineering Co. Ltd.* v. *Crown*,[70]
    (iii) in practice the employee is regarded as being continuously
          employed,
    (iv) pregnancy (up to 26 weeks maximum) unless the employee
         returns to work within 29 weeks of the week of confinement.

---

[69] E.P.C.A. 1978 s.49.
[70] [1976] I.R.L.R. 146.

TERMINATION

The employee is aided by the fact there is a legal presumption that continuous employment exists.[71]

6.61   Finally where strikes/lockouts occur the weeks will not count towards the two year figure, but will not break continuity. The rules provide that the period from the last working day to the first working day after industrial action should be counted. Thus weekends (assuming the strike continues over a weekend) will be deducted from an employee's total length of service.

6.62   If there is a change of employer this may not break continuity of employment. The common law position is that a transfer to a new employer would breach the continuity provisions.[72] However (by virtue of E.P.C.A. Sched. 13, para. 17) a transfer of a business trade or undertaking (as opposed to a sale of the company's assets) or a transfer to an associated employer will not break continuity. An associated employer is one which is either a company which directly or indirectly is a holding or subsidiary company of the other party, or they are both subsidiaries of a third company. Control means voting control, (*i.e.* 51 per cent. of the votes). Please see Chapter 9 for details on the Regulations affecting transfers of business.

6.63   Note that if an employee alleges unfair dismissal for trade union reasons, (*i.e.* intention to join or take part in activities or membership of a trade union at an appropriate time or refusal to join a trade union) the employee need not be under the normal retirement age or have had two years continuous employment.

Excluded Classes

6.64 The main excluded classes of employees are:

(a) Registered dock workers.
(b) Crew men serving certain fishing vessels.
(c) Employees who work outside the United Kingdom (the courts will look to where the employee has his base).[73]
(d) Employees over the age of retirement.[74] The law in this area has been affected by the Sex Discrimination Act 1986. There are two

---

[71] See E.P.C.A. 1978 s.151.
[72] See *Nokes* v. *Doncaster Amalgamated Collieries Ltd.* [1940] 3 All E.R. 549.
[73] See *Wilson* v. *Maynard* [1978] I.C.R. 376 and also *Wood* v. *Cunard Line, The Times,* April 7, 1989.
[74] E.P.C.A. 1978 s.641(b).

questions to be asked. First, is there a normal retiring age, common to both men and women for the job in question? (It will normally but not necessarily be the contractual retiring age). If so, and the employee has exceeded this age then the employee cannot bring a claim for unfair dismissal. The retiring age must be common to both men and women. The normal retiring age is the age at which employees can normally expect to be required to retire. If there is no common retirement age then the age limit for both men and women is 65.

Dismissal

Reference has already been made to E.P.C.A. 1978 s.55 which **6.65** defines "dismissal" for unfair dismissal purposes. This includes termination by the employer with or without notice, non renewal of fixed term contracts and finally termination by the employee in circumstances where he is entitled to do so by the employers conduct (constructive dismissal).

Constructive Dismissal

Constructive dismissal has already been referred to but requires **6.66** further explanation. Section 55 has been interpreted in *Western Excavating (E.C.C.) Ltd.* v. *Sharp*[75] in which the Court of Appeal held that the employee is entitled to terminate only where the employer is guilty of a repudiatory breach of contract, or evinces an intention no longer to be bound by the contract. The breach must be serious enough to entitle the employee to leave immediately. Indeed Lord Denning said that he should do so. This is not a strict rule and if the employee "marks the card" he may stay on under protest for some time.

However, whilst a breach of an express term may be easy to identify, **6.67** as indicated above, the courts have also accepted that repudiatory

---

[75] [1978] I.C.R. 221.

breaches of implied terms may give good grounds for constructive dismissal. Thus in *British Aircraft Corp.* v. *Austin*[76] breach of the employer's implied duty to take reasonable steps to care for the employee entitled the employee to resign. This was an early attempt to water down the effect of the strict contractual approach of *Western Excavating* (see above). The courts have also accepted that a term can be applied into contracts that there should be mutual trust and confidence between the parties. This term can be very difficult to identify and in particular when and how it is broken. By introducing and expanding the concept of constructive dismissal for breach of implied terms the tribunals have sought further to reduce the impact of the strict contractual test laid down by the Court of Appeal in *Western Excavating* which was making (and indeed still does) cases much more difficult for applicants in tribunals.

Effective Date of Termination

6.68   Reference has been made to the "effective date of termination" (E.D.T.) which is defined in E.P.C.A., s.55. This is a crucial date in that the employee must have been employed for two years by the E.D.T. and his claim to an industrial tribunal for unfair dismissal must be made within three months of the E.D.T. There is a residual discretion in the industrial tribunal to extend the deadline for bringing a claim where it was not reasonably practicable to do so.[77] The exception has been narrowly construed. Compare, however, *Dedman* v. *British Building and Engineering Appliances Ltd.*,[78] when the Court of Appeal said that if the applicant or his advisors were not at fault in allowing the time limit to pass then it could be within the scope of the exception. Ignorance of one's rights is not a sufficient reason for delay *Avon County Council* v. *Haywood Hicks*.[79]

6.69   It is important that dismissal letters are worded carefully since what is said may affect the E.D.T. (albeit unintentionally). Thus in *Chapman* v. *Letheby & Christopher Ltd.*[80] a letter dismissing an employee, contained

---

[76] [1978] I.R.L.R. 332.
[77] E.P.C.A. 1978 s.67(2).
[78] [1974] I.C.R. 53.
[79] [1983] I.R.L.R. 171.
[80] [1981] I.R.L.R. 440.

an inherent contradiction, describing the lump sum payment as payment in lieu, but also referring to the date notice was due to expire. If the employer's contention was correct then the employee's claim was out of time. The tribunal stated that the employee rightly relied on the reference to the specific date in the letter. Furthermore even if this were not so then the tribunal felt that ambiguities in a dismissal letter should be construed against the employer. Letters will be construed on the basis of an ordinary reasonable employees understanding.

If an employee appeals against his summary dismissal, the E.D.T. is **6.70** the date he was dismissed, not the date which the appeal confirms the decision to dismiss; *e.g.* in *Sainsbury* v. *Savage*,[81] and confirmed in *West Midlands* v. *Tipton*.[82] In *Cooke* v. *Ministry of Defence* the works rules provided that the dismissal be postponed until the appeal had been concluded. The court held this did not affect the rule in *Sainsbury* v. *Savage*.

The E.D.T. will be delayed by a week in certain circumstances if the employee has been given less than his statutory minimum notice under section 49 (see also paragraph 6.48 above).

"Fair" Reasons for Dismissal

An employer must show that the reason for dismissal comes within **6.71** one of the five "fair" reasons for dismissal. If he does not then the dismissal will be unfair.[83] The five reasons are:

(a) relating to the capability or the qualifications of the employee for performing work of the kind which he was employed to do;

(b) relating to the conduct of the employee;

(c) that the employee was redundant;

(d) that the employee could not continue to work in the position which he held without contravention of the duty or restriction imposed by or under an enactment;

(e) some other substantial reason of a kind such as to justify the dismissal of an employee holding the position which that employee held.

---

[81] [1980] I.R.L.R. 104.
[82] [1986] I.R.L.R. 112
[83] *Raynor* v. *Remploy Ltd.* [1973] I.R.L.R. 3.

6.72 The tribunal, having decided that the employer has showed that the reason was one of the above reasons will proceed to consider whether the dismissal was fair in all the circumstances, having regard to "equity and the substantial merits of the case."[84] The tribunal will have regard to the size of the administrative resources of the employer.

6.73 There are two aspects to a dismissal, which broadly speaking must both be satisfactory, substantive and procedural aspects. In other words not only may an employee be, say, lacking in capability, but the employer must show that the procedure by which the employee was dismissed, was fair. The procedural side, which previously had been down-graded in importance, has been re-emphasised by the House of Lords in *Polkey* v. *Dayton (A.E.) Services*[85] and therefore practically speaking it is wise for employers to err on the side of caution in this respect. The action of an employer in treating the reason as a sufficient reason for dismissal will include at least part of the manner of dismissal.

"Reasonableness" of Dismissal

6.74 The tribunal must decide whether the employer's actions fitted into the band of reasonable responses reasonable employers would have chosen.[86]

The employee's decision to dismiss must be reasonable both at the time he dismisses and the time the decision is confirmed at an appeal stage.[87]

Whilst at common law[88] the employer could rely on conduct unknown to him at the time of the dismissal but discovered later, this cannot be a fair basis for a dismissal under statute.[89] Conversely matters which come to light after an appeal that has been heard, will not retroactively render the decision unfair.[90]

---

[84] E.P.C.A. 1978 s.57(3).
[85] [1987] I.R.L.R. 503.
[86] See *British Leyland (U.K.) Ltd.* v. *Swift* [1981] I.R.L.R. 91.
[87] See *West Midland Co-operative Society* v. *Tipton* [1986] 1 All E.R. 513.
[88] See *Boston Deep Sea Fishing* v. *Ansell* [1888] 39 Ch.D. 339.
[89] See *Devis W. & Sons* v. *Atkins* [1977] I.R.L.R. 314.
[90] See *Greenall Whitley* v. *Carr* [1985] I.R.L.R. 289.

Automatically Unfair Reasons for Dismissal

In deciding whether the decision making process was fair, the **6.75** tribunal may have regard to the A.C.A.S. Codes of Practice and therefore it is necessary for employers to take these into account when deciding on their disciplinary procedures. Finally it should be noted that there are certain reasons which are automatically unfair reasons.

(a) If an employee is dismissed in connection with a transfer of business and the fact that the transfer is the main or principal reason for the dismissal, the dismissal will be unfair by virtue of the Transfer of Undertakings (Protection of Employees) Regulations 1981 unless the employer can show that it was for an economic, technical or organisational reason entailing changes in the work force. If this is the case then the decision would be judged as if it was "some other substantial reason" for unfair dismissal purposes and an employer will have to produce evidence of its reasonableness.

(b) If a woman is dismissed for pregnancy, the dismissal will be automatically unfair unless she was incapable of performing her job adequately or she could not continue to do her job without contravention of statute. However for an employer to rely on this argument he must show that there was no alternative job which could have been offered to her which was suitable and substantially less favourable to her. The burden of showing this is on the employer.[91]

(c) If an employee is dismissed for joining or intending to join a trade union, or for taking part in trade union activities at an appropriate time or refusing to become a trade union member then this dismissal will be automatically unfair.[92] It has already been pointed out that employees in this situation do not have to have two years continuous employment or be under the retiring age.

---

[91] E.P.C.A. 1978 s.6
[92] E.P.C.A. 1978 s.58.

TERMINATION

Calculating the Employee's Award

6.76   Should an employee be successful at an industrial tribunal, then (subject to any deductions the industrial tribunal may make) his award will be in two parts. The basic award is calculated by reference to a statutory formula. This is a multiplier × length continuous service × wage. The multiplier will be half for each year in which the employee is below 22 years old, will be one for each year that the employee is below 41 but over 21 and one and a half for each year thereafter. There is a maximum of 20 years which an employee can count. Thus if an employee is 35, and has worked since 18, (*i.e.* 17 years) he will be able to claim three times half a week's wage, plus fourteen times one week's wage. Over 64 the amount is reduced by 1/12 for each month that the employer is nearer to 65. For men over 64, and women over 59, the award is reduced by 12 for each completed month of service after their 64th and 59th birthdays respectively.

The current maximum is £172 per week. The current maximum basic award is therefore £5,160.

6.77   The basic award can be reduced for the following reasons[93]

   (a) the conduct of the applicant prior to dismissal was such that it is just and equitable to reduce the award;
   (b) the applicant has unreasonably refused an offer of reinstatement;
   (c) if an employer has paid any redundancy pay then this would be offset against the basic award;
   (d) Any industrial tribunal may, if they expressly state reduce or extinguish the basic award.[94]

6.78   A compensatory award can be made by the tribunal which is the sum which is just and equitable in the circumstances having regard to any loss sustained by the applicant in consequence of and in so far as the loss is attributable to the action taken by the employers. This will cover loss of wages up to the industrial tribunal hearing, loss of wages after the industrial tribunal hearing, (*i.e.* the tribunal will estimate how long it will take the employee to get a job) loss of statutory rights, loss of pension rights and loss of perks, and the expenses of looking for new work.

---

[93] E.P.C A. 1978 s.73.
[94] See *Chelsea Football and Athletic Club* v. *Heath* [1981] I.C.R. 323.

The tribunal will then make the following deductions: **6.79**

(a) The common law duty of an employee to mitigate loss which has already been referred to—it is expressly retained for unfair dismissal cases[95]
(b) any conduct of the employee in causing or contributing to the dismissal—the conduct of the employee must be blameworthy in some way.[96]

It has been held that payments in lieu of notice should be deducted from the compensatory award.[97]

The compensatory award is subject to a current maximum of £8,925. The maximum is applied after the loss has been assessed and any deductions have been made.[98]

Special awards can be made where it is decided that an employee was unfairly dismissed for trade union reasons (defined above) and the applicant has requested reinstatement or re-engagement.

If no order for reinstatment/re-engagement is made the award will be **6.80** 104 weeks pay, or £12,550 whichever is the greater up to a maximum of £25,040 special award is made in addition to the basic and compensatory awards.

If the employer does not comply with the special award then this is increased to £18,795 or 156 weeks pay whichever is the greater. The employer can argue either when the special award is made for the first time, or on enforcement that it is not practical for him to take the employee back.

Reinstatement or Re-engagement

Although these are supposedly the primary remedies[99] they are rarely **6.81** ordered. Reinstatement is an order that the employer shall treat the applicant as if he had never been dismissed. The tribunal make any supplementary order regarding benefits payable to the applicant.

---

[95] E.P.C.A. 1978 s.74(4).
[96] See *Nelson* v. *BBC (No. 2)* [1979] I.R.L.R. 346; reductions of 100 per cent. have been known: *Devis & Sons Ltd.* v. *Atkins* [1977] I.R.L.R. 314.
[97] See *Addison* v. *Babcock F.A.T.A. Ltd.* [1987] 2 All E.R. 784.
[98] See *McCarthy* v. *British Insulated Callendars Cables plc* [1985] I.R.L.R. 94.
[99] E.P.C.A. 1978 ss.68, 69.

TERMINATION

Re-engagement is an order that the employer (or an associated or successor employer) will re-employ the applicant on comparable or suitable terms. The tribunal must consider reinstatement first.[1]

If the award made is only partially complied with the tribunal may make an order awarding such compensation as the tribunal thinks fit. If the order is made and not complied with at all then, unless the employer convinces the tribunal that it was not practicable to comply with the order an additional award will be made. This will be between 13 and 26 weeks pay unless the reason for the dismissal was sexual or racial discrimination in which case it will be between 26 and 52 weeks pay. A weeks pay is subject to the statutory maximum of £172.

Costs in Cases of Unilateral Termination

6.82   Costs will in general not be awarded to either party. However if the applicant[2] is guilty of frivolous, vexatious or otherwise unreasonable conduct, costs may be awarded. This does not cover conduct in front of the tribunal.[3]

Appeals

Appeals on a point of law may be made to the Employment Appeal Tribunal within 42 days of the document recording the decision being sent to the appellant. Before the E.A.T. can overturn an I.T. decision it must have been wrong in law, either expressly or by virtue of having reached a decision which no reasonable industrial tribunal could possibly have reached, if it had properly directed itself. In *Neale* v. *Hereford & Worcester County Council*[4] the Court of Appeal said that appellate tribunal should not substitute its decision as to the right course for that of the employer. In every case there is a band of

---

[1] Under E.P.C.A. 1978 s.69.
[2] Or the employer: see *Davidson* v. *John Calder* [1985] I.C.R. 143.
[3] See *O'Keefe* v. *Southampton County Council* [1988] I.C.R. 419.
[4] [1986] I.C.R. 471.

reasonable responses to an employee's conduct, a dismissal is only unfair if the decision to dismiss falls outside that band.

Injunctions

Traditionally the Courts have not allowed an employee to argue that **6.83** his contract of employment may not be terminated, and to enforce this right by an injunction or by an order that the contract be continued (specific performance). In *Ridge* v. *Baldwin*[5] it was said "there cannot be specific performance of a contract of service". Three reasons are usually put forward. The Court will not impose a contract of slavery; usually there is a lack of continuing confidence between the parties and, therefore, there would be the need for constant supervision. However where these objections can be avoided (for instance a mere assertion of a lack of confidence will not suffice; see *Powell* v. *London Borough of Brent*[6]) employees have, in special circumstances, been able to obtain injunctions until proper contractual procedures for the dismissal have been carried out. In *Hill* v. *Parsons*[7] the employee was dismissed because of trade union pressure. The Courts were prepared to grant an injunction (although the fact that the injunction would allow the employee to take advantage of the passage of the Industrial Relations Act is often cited as an exceptional factor).

In general it appears that employees will only be able to obtain **6.84** injunctions in circumstances where there is inadequate notice or where an employer has conducted himself in a particular way outside the terms of the contract. Thus in *McClelland* v. *Northern Ireland General Health Services Board*[8] the House of Lords granted an injunction where an employer had provided that the contract could only be terminated on certain grounds, when notwithstanding this he thereupon proceeded to terminate the contract on a different ground (see also *Irani* v. *Southampton & South West Hampshire Area Health Authority*[9] where Warner J. said damages would have been an inadequate remedy because the applicant would not have been able to work in the N.H.S. again).

If an employee can deal with the three standard objections referred to **6.85** above then he or she may be able to look for an interlocutory injunction. The basic principles were laid down in *American Cyanamid* v. *Ethicon*.[10]

---

[5] [1964] A.C. 40.
[6] [1987] I.R.L.R. 467.
[7] [1971] 3 All E.R. 1345.
[8] [1957] 2 All E.R. 139.
[9] [1985] I.R.L.R. 203.
[10] [1975] A.C. 396.

TERMINATION

These were:

   (a) the applicant must have an arguable case;
   (b) damages would not be an adequate remedy;
   (c) the balance of convenience favours the grant of an injunction.

Employers may often find difficulty in (b).

The Court of Appeal has suggested that employment cases are slightly different and that the balance is the balance of the risk of doing an injustice rather than inconvenience. It is submitted that, notwithstanding, the *American Cyanmid* principles still apply to employment cases.

Judicial Review

6.86   The Courts in the past have been prepared to grant judicial review in relation to dismissal by public bodies. Decisions taken by such bodies can broadly be challenged on the grounds that they are not in accordance with statute, there has been procedural impropriety, (*i.e.* breach of natural justice) and that the decision is "outrageous" in that no sensible person could have reached that particular decision.[11]

6.87   However since *R.* v. *East Berkshire Health Authority*[12] the courts have adopted a very strict policy towards judicial review stating that "mere" employees are covered by the unfair dismissal provisions and therefore their employment in the public sector alone does not qualify them to use public law remedies. Mr Walsh for instance was a very senior nursing officer who wished to allege that his dismissal was invalid for procedural impropriety. The Court of Appeal, overturning the first instance Judge said "the ordinary employer is free to act in breach of the contract of employment but if he does so the employee will acquire certain private law rights and remedies". If there are special statutory restrictions on the employer (*i.e.* statutory bodies) this may be sufficient to allow the employee to use public law rights. Compare this with *Ridge* v. *Baldwin*.[13]

If the Court decides that an application for judicial review should not be allowed then it may allow the proceedings to continue as if they had been started by writ.[14] The practical effect of this will be to turn an application for judicial review into an action claiming damages for breach of contract.

---

[11] See *R.* v. *The Secretary of State for Foreign and Commonwealth Affairs, ex p. Council of Civil Service Unions: The G.C.H.Q. case* [1985] I.R.L.R. 28.
[12] *Ex p. Walsh* [1984] I.C.R. 426.
[13] [1963] 2 All E.R. 66.
[14] R.S.C. Ord. 53(9).

Post-Termination

Confidential Information

The case of *Faccenda* v. *Fowler*[15] referred to in paragraph 3.14 above **6.88** sets out very clearly the relevant and current state of the law on confidential information and the ability of the employer to restrain employees post termination from improperly disseminating information confidential to their former employer.

Restraining Employee From Working For Competing Enterprises

The old cases suggested in relation to implied terms that there was no **6.89** general duty to provide work and that the "master" fulfilled his obligation to his "servant" by paying wages. There was, however, a gloss upon this general statement, if the opportunity to work was of the essence of the contract. Public performers could claim damages for loss of the opportunity of enhancing their reputation by publicity—actors[16] and the editor of a newspaper could claim damages if its publication was discontinued.[17] Also where an employee was paid by commission, he had to be given the opportunity of earning such commission. In *Evening Standard Co.* v. *Hendersen*[18] the Court of Appeal, in effect, endorsed the sending home of the employee by granting an injunction to restrain the Evening Standard's production manager from working for a rival newspaper during his notice period. The company undertook to pay Mr. Hendersen wages during the notice period and to continue to employ him as a production manager if he so wished. This type of restraint has become known colloquially as "garden leave" and it has become particularly significant in the City of London in the musical chairs that has taken place leading up to and subsequent to Big Bang.

---

[15] [1986] I.C.R. 2978.
[16] See *Clayton and Waller Ltd.* v. *Oliver* [1930] All E.R. 44.
[17] See *Collier* v. *Sunday Referee Publishing Co. Ltd.* [1940] 4 All E.R. 234.
[18] [1987] I.R.L.R. 64.

"Garden leave" injunctions

6.90   In *Provident Financial Group plc and Whitegates Estate Agency Ltd.*
v. *Hayward*[19] the Court of Appeal upheld the Judge's refusal to grant an
injunction to restrain Provident Financial Group's former finance director
from joining a competitor before his notice period had expired. They
did, however, say that an injunction could, in certain circumstances, be
granted.

They confirmed that a "garden leave" injunction could be granted in
appropriate cases but held in that case that the Judge was justified in
refusing to grant the injunction since the plaintiffs were unlikely to suffer
significant damage if the defendant started working for a competitor
three months before his notice period came to an end. It seemed to be
significant that the plaintiffs could not really point to a legitimate
business interest they were seeking to protect against Mr Hayward
since it appeared on the facts that he was going to be carrying out
rather different activities than he had been carrying out for them and
that there would be unlikely to be breaches of confidence, *etc.*

6.91   Mr. Hayward was employed by Whitegates Estate Agency Ltd., a
wholly owned subsidiary of the Provident Financial Group, as financial
controller and finance director and his contract provided that he was
not, unless otherwise previously agreed in writing, to

> "undertake any other business of profession or be or become an
> employee or agent of any other person or persons or assist or have any
> financial interest in any other business or profession".

He also undertook to

> "carry out his duties in a proper, loyal and efficient manner and to use his
> best endeavours to promote the interests and reputation of the company
> and not to do anything which is harmful to them".[20]

On July 1, 1988, he gave in his notice and it was subsequently agreed
that the period of notice should be reduced to six months. As part of the
agreement he undertook not to disclose any confidential information
about the company for a period of two years from July 1. He actually
stopped working on September 5 but was paid up to December 31. On
October 13 he wrote to the second plaintiffs informing them that he

---

[19] [1989] I.R.L.R. 84.
[20] Paraphrase of the contract.

proposed to start working for Asda from October 17. The Judge held that he was not satisfied that an injunction would be granted if the matter proceeded to trial and concluded that it was not an appropriate case for an interlocutory injunction. On appeal the plaintiffs argued that the present case was on all fours with *Evening Standard* v. *Hendersen* and the objection raised by the courts to an injunction on the basis that it would amount to specific performance of the contract did not apply.

Mr. Hayward argued that Hendersen was wrong and should not be applied because his obligations were expressed in a negative form, that is to say not to undertake other work and enforcement would result in a positive obligation to work for the plaintiffs. The Court disagreed pointing out that the wording was common and there was nothing to prevent the Court from granting an injunction in an appropriate case, although as it happens not in his case. Clearly the willingness to pay until the notice period expired was relevant, as was the willingness to offer work during that period, but what seemed crucial was whether the proposed new employment was likely seriously to damage the existing employer's business.

It shows the enormous importance of ensuring that the correct issues **6.92** are dealt with in affidavits in support of applications for an injunction. If, for example, it is said that public interest requires that the employee should be entitled to work for whom he pleases, it may be worth the employer exploring on affidavit precisely what the alleged public interest is. The old cases referred to above were decided some many years ago and it is submitted that the public interest has moved on and changed since those days.

CHAPTER 7

MATERNITY

Introduction

Many employers regard a pregnant employee as an inconvenience and **7.1**
would prefer to plan their employment requirements on the basis that
the employee will not be returning; future shortages of recruits may
force them to reassess their needs and positively to encourage
employees who have been on maternity leave to return to work.

On any view the law relating to maternity pay and maternity leave is **7.2**
complex; it is governed not only by the E.P.C.A. but also by the Social
Security Acts of 1975 and 1986 ('S.S.A. 1975 and 1986'), the Statutory
Maternity Pay (General) Regulations 1986 (S.I. 1986, No. 1960) ('S.M.P.
regulations') and by other regulations. There has been a plea by at least
one president of the EAT for the regulations to be simplified and they
have been compared unfavourably to tax statutory instruments. Broadly
the aim of the S.M.P. regulations is to follow the statutory sick pay rules
and regulations and there are some aspects of the two regulations
which overlap.

Appendix 6 sets out the latest sums which should be paid under the
S.M.P. regulations.

Essentially an employee's rights are governed by statute, but it is **7.3**
possible for the contract to affect the statutory position providing it does
not seek to reduce the rights an employee has under statute. Section 48
of E.P.C.A. permits an employee to have a composite right and to select
and enforce the right which is most favourable to her. A composite right
is one where the employee has rights not only under E.P.C.A. but also
under her contract of employment. Employers must be extremely
careful in making any contractual arrangements with employees and

must set out the position to the employee clearly in writing. In *Lucas* v. *Norton of London Ltd.*,[1] Lucas had no statutory right to return to work but there was what was described as a "nebulous agreement" that she might return to work having had her baby and she was paid the equivalent of maternity pay when she left. When she endeavoured to return to work she was told that there was no job available and she was paid two weeks' pay "in lieu of notice." On the facts it was found that the contract was varied to allow for unpaid leave of absence, that the contract continued in her absence and that the payment in lieu of notice was evidence of acceptance by the employer of the variation.

Statutory Maternity Pay

7.4 The entitlement to statutory maternity pay arises under section 46 of S.S.A. 1986. There are five conditions which an employee should satisfy before she becomes entitled to be paid S.M.P.

(a) She has been continuously employed for a period of at least 26 weeks ending with the week immediately preceding the 14th week before the expected week of confinement ('E.W.C.').

(b) Her normal weekly earnings for the period of eight weeks ending with the week immediately preceding the 14th week before the E.W.C. are not less than the lower earning limits for paying National Insurance Contributions.

(c) That she has given notice at least 21 days before her absence from work to the person who is liable to pay S.M.P. that she is going to be absent from work wholly or partly because of pregnancy or confinement or later if it is not reasonably practical to do so.

(d) At least 21 days beforehand she must produce medical evidence of the E.W.C.

(e) She must stop work.

---

[1] [1984] I.R.L.R. 86.

7.5 The E.W.C. is the week when the baby is due and the qualifying week ('Q.W.') put simply is the 15th week before the E.W.C. It should be noted that S.M.P. is not payable earlier than the 11th week before the E.W.C. even if the employee has stopped work beforehand. If the employee is dismissed by the employer after she has eight weeks' continuous employment and but for that dismissal she would have acquired 26 weeks' employment and the reason for the dismissal was to avoid S.M.P., she shall be deemed to have worked for 26 continuous weeks and will receive S.M.P.

7.6 There are two rates for S.M.P. In order to be paid the higher rate S.M.P. an employee must have worked for two continuous years ending with the Q.W. providing she has worked at least 16 hours weekly under the contract of employment for two years, or five years ending with the Q.W. if the employee has worked between eight and 16 hours weekly.[2] The entitlement to higher rate S.M.P. is not lost by an employee who has two years' continuous employment if for no more than 26 weeks she works between eight and 16 hours.

To be entitled to the lower rate, a woman only has to work for 26 continuous weeks and whilst there is no requirement to show any particular number of hours worked in each week the employee must show an average weekly earning at least equal to the National Insurance Contributions.

The maternity pay period over which S.M.P. is payable totals 18 weeks. Assuming an employee is entitled to the higher rate then the employee receives the higher rate for six weeks and the lower rate for the balance. The earliest S.M.P. can be paid is the 11th week before the E.W.C. but payment cannot commence any later than the 6th week before the E.W.C. Consequently if a woman chooses to work beyond the 6th week she will lose some weeks' S.M.P.

The higher rate is paid at 90 per cent. of the average weekly earning and the lower rate is fixed from time to time by statutory instrument.

Right to return to work

7.7 This is dealt with by E.P.C.A., ss.33 and 45–48.

An employee is entitled to return to work providing she continues to be employed by her employer (whether or not she is at work) until immediately before the beginning of the 11th week before the E.W.C.

---

[2] S.S.A. 1986, s.48.

provided that at that time she has been continuously employed for a period of not less than two years. She is also required to inform her employer at least 21 days before her absence begins, or if that is not reasonably practicable then as soon as it is reasonably practicable that:

(a) she will be absent from work wholly or partly because of pregnancy or confinement;
(b) she intends to work with her employer; and
(c) The E.W.C., or, if confinement has already taken place, the date of confinement.

Notice of Intention to Return to Work

7.8   In order to return to work under section 47 she must give notice of her intention to return in writing to the employer, at least 21 days before the date on which she proposes to return. The employer can, under section 33, not earlier than 49 days after the beginning of the E.W.C., request an employee to give written confirmation of the intention to return to work and there must be a response by the employee within 14 days of the request. The importance of time limits generally in relation to maternity cannot be stressed too strongly. Time and time again an employee will lose her statutory right to return and sometimes any contractual right by a failure to comply with those time limits.

Postponing the Return to Work

7.9   There are rights for both the employer and the employee to postpone the return to work. Assuming there is no interruption of work, the employer may postpone an employee's return to work by no more than four weeks from the notified date of return providing he notifies her before that date that for specified reasons he is postponing her return.

7.10   Likewise the employee may postpone her date of return by no more than four weeks from the notified date of return notwithstanding such postponement extends her time for return beyond the 29 weeks. However section 47(4) of E.P.C.A. permits just one postponement. It would appear that if after that time the employee cannot return to work then the employment terminates. There is no dismissal and so all rights are lost; see *Kelly* v. *Liverpool Maritime Chemicals Ltd.*[3] Note it may still be possible under the contract to allow more than one postponement.

Under section 45 the employee has the right to return to work in the **7.11** job in which she was employed under the original contract of employment and on terms and conditions not less favourable than those which would have applied to her if she had not been absent. Such terms and conditions include seniority, pension rights and similar rights and there has been some debate as to what happens to benefits such as pension rights during the period of absence. E.P.C.A. is of little assistance; Schedule 2, paragraph 6 and section 48 accept that a contract can subsist during the period of absence, but if one looks at paragraphs 9 and 13 of Schedule 13, whilst they permit continuity of employment it is clear from those paragraphs that the contract of employment will not necessarily subsist during that time. Again this may be something which ought to be dealt with in the contract.

Contract of Employment

Demographic statistics suggest there will be a shortage of employees **7.12** and experienced staff who are familiar with the employer and its operations are a valuable asset. For that reason many employers have settled upon a policy which will encourage staff to return even if they have not fulfilled the basic statutory requirements of service.

Nevertheless, whether or not an employer intends to grant to an **7.13** employee enhanced rights it is submitted that it would be sensible for an employer as a matter of practice to have a formal policy. Career breaks for longer than the statutory periods are well worth consideration also.

An employer may well feel that he does not intend to continue, *inter alia*, pension benefits, use of the company car, *etc.,* during the period of absence but if that is his view then he would be wise specifically to state this in writing. It is where there is a failure to state the position in writing that confusion can arise and that is just one step away from a hearing before a tribunal.

It is not merely in the area of benefits that an employer should set out **7.14** clearly the contractual position. As is said above, section 48 recognises that there can be a composite right. An employer may be prepared to

---

[3] [1988] I.R.L.R. 310.

pay more than the statutory maternity pay or allow a longer period of absence for maternity leave and providing the employer is not trying to reduce the statutory right the employee will then be able to select the contractual right in preference to the statutory entitlement. Where the contract fails to state what the entitlement is, the court will imply that the statutory right is available. For example in *Lavery* v. *Plessey Telecommunications Ltd*.[4] Lavery had a right to return to work but failed to give the correct notice exercising her statutory right. She claimed she also had a contractual right to return to work but there was no evidence that this varied the statutory notice requirements and it was held that in the absence of any specific provision it must be assumed that the contractual right was the same as the statutory right. Consequently Lavery lost not only her statutory right to return to work but also the contractual right.

7.15 It is probably impractical for an employer to include the company policy in the contract of employment. The employer will nevertheless want to make it clear that the company does have a policy which will apply to the employee should she become pregnant. It is suggested that there should be a clear statement in the contract which refers to the company's policy. A form of wording which may suffice would be as follows:

> "Should you become pregnant you may be entitled to statutory maternity pay and maternity leave. The company is committed to a policy of encouraging employees to return to work, even if they only want to return on a part-time basis, and has therefore adopted a policy which not only encompasses statutory requirements in respect of pregnant employees but also enhanced rights for the employees. A copy of the company policy which forms a part of your terms and conditions of employment can be obtained on request from the personnel manager."

7.16 Employers may recognise that an employee wants to return to work but is unable to do so full time. If the employer is willing to permit a return to work on a part-time basis then the terms and conditions should be fully set out. Remember if the employee has two years' continuous employment and she returns to work on a part-time basis it cannot be assumed that she now has to acquire five years' continuous employment to be afforded E.P.C.A. protection. The employee comes within E.P.C.A. rights as she has completed two years' continuous employment.

Appendix 7 contains some general headings which should be borne in mind when preparing a policy.

---

[4] [1988] I.R.L.R. 202.

Discrimination

Employers should be careful that they do not fall foul of the Sex **7.17** Discrimination Act 1975 ('S.D.A.'). If an employee who has not attained the requisite continuous employment seeks to return to work after the birth of her child and the employer refuses to take her back the employer may be faced with a claim for unfair dismissal. *Turley* v. *Alders Department Stores Ltd.*[5] suggests that a claim could not be brought, but more recent cases *Hayes* v. *Malleable Working Men's Club*[6] and *Maughan* v. *North East London Magistrates Committee*[7] did not follow *Turley*. While *Turley* has not been overturned the EAT has accepted that there is no principle of law preventing a tribunal from applying the Sex Discrimination Act. A recent example of this was the unreported case of *Curl* v. *Air U.K. Ltd.*[8] In that case Curl asked for four weeks' unpaid maternity leave and this was refused because it was company policy not to allow a woman to return if she did not qualify for the statutory right. An attempt was made to persuade Curl to sign a form saying she had terminated her own employment which she declined to do and the tribunal found that she had not terminated her employment but had been dismissed. In that case the tribunal compared Curl's situation with that of a man injured in a rugby match who asked for four weeks off in order to recover. Evidently the employers admitted that a male employee would be allowed such time off and the tribunal decided the company policy on pregnant women without statutory rights not being allowed to return whatever the individual circumstances applied solely to women and, as there was no comparable position with regard to men, Curl's claim was therefore upheld.

This suggests that the employers' task is becoming more complex and that the tribunal is taking a much more sympathetic approach to the employee.

The tribunal's finding might well have been different were it not for the **7.18** fact that Curl wanted time off in order to have the baby and then return to work once she was fit for work. What it does mean, however, is that when an employer is considering dismissing a pregnant employee for some reason connected with her pregnancy, the employer cannot rely solely on the fact that she has insufficient continuity of service to defeat an unfair dismissal claim as there may be possible claims under the Sex Discrimination Act 1975.

---

[5] [1980] I.R.L.R. 4.
[6] [1985] I.C.R. 703, EAT.
[7] [1985] I.R.L.R. 367, EAT.
[8] C.O.I.T. 1987 Folio No. 3/116/158.

MATERNITY

Discrimination and Part-time Employees

7.19   Discrimination problems arise in respect of part-time employment. In *Home Office* v. *Holmes*[9] it was held that the requirement that a woman at a particular grade and department be full-time was discriminatory as only a smaller proportion of women could comply with that requirement, namely to be a full-time employee. There has been a contrasting case: *Greater Glasgow Health Board* v. *Carey*[10] where Mrs. Carey before she took maternity leave was a full-time health worker and on her return only wanted to work part-time. The Board was prepared to accept part-time work on the basis of five-day working (either morning or afternoon) which was not accepted by Mrs. Carey. The EAT held that the administrative efficiency of the service was a justifiable reason under the S.D.A. for this discrimination. This is a Scottish case and might not necessarily be followed to the letter in the English EAT. Further it would be dangerous to assume that *Holmes* (see above) was a one-off case. If the employee prior to maternity leave worked full-time but was permitted to return part-time, an attempt then to impose, at a later date, full-time working may be discriminatory. Arguably, this problem could be overcome by a consensual amendment or variation to the contract of employment.

---

[9] [1985] 1 W.L.R. 71.
[10] [1987] I.R.L.R. 484.

CHAPTER 8

SICK PAY

Introduction

The law in relation to Statutory Sick Pay ('S.S.P.') is set out in the Social **8.1**
Security and Housing Benefits Act 1982 ('the 1982 Act') which has been
amended in certain respects by the Social Security Act 1985 and the
principal regulations are the Statutory Sick Pay (General) Regulations
1982, (S.I. 1982, No. 894) ('the General Regulations'). One commentator
has observed that the legislation is drafted by civil servants for civil
servants and, as seems to be customary with social security legislation,
enabling powers are given. Consequently, the rules and regulations
seem to be made up as they go along and in parts are almost
unintelligible.

The Department of Health and Social Security has issued an **8.2**
employer's guide to S.S.P. which is lengthy but does provide employers
with answers to the sort of questions that an employer might have to
face from time to time on the type of documentation which has to be
retained and from whom an employer can recover money in the event of
an overpayment. The amounts that can be paid are varied annually by
statutory instrument.

Regulation 13 of the General Regulations lays down legal require- **8.3**
ments for employers to maintain records such as:

(a) date of sickness absences in the tax year lasting four or more
    days;
(b) date of sickness absences for which S.S.P. was not paid to the
    employee;
(c) the reason why S.S.P. was not paid;
(d) details of the agreed qualifying days in each period of
    entitlement.

Occupational Sick Pay

8.4   As in many other areas of employment law the statutory position can be enhanced by the contract of employment although the rights which accrue under legislation cannot be eroded by the contract of employment. (The records which have to be maintained under Regulation 13 may be used as part of the employer's record if the employer chooses to offer enhanced sick pay terms and conditions.)

Sickness is an emotive area and for that reason it is important not to rely upon an oral promise. This is especially important where there is a question of occupational sick pay. It is far better to have the rules and regulations laid down in writing in a formal occupational sick pay scheme for the avoidance of doubt, particularly if the employer wishes to consider taking disciplinary action in the event of continual ill health or absence.

8.5   There is some academic debate as to the extent of any non-statutory obligation on an employer to pay wages during a period of ill health. If pay is in consideration of actual work undertaken, then a sick employee will not be paid for the period of absence. In theory unless there is an agreement to the contrary an employer, by implication anyway, agrees to pay for service only and at common law an employee who does not work is therefore not entitled to any wages. In reality there is likely to be some agreement and if there is nothing either expressly or impliedly agreed, custom and practice may indicate what the actual position is. As indicated above, the leading modern authority on this issue is *Mears* v. *Safecar Security Ltd.*[1] which also contains some interesting observations generally about section 11 of E.P.C.A. (which enables an employee to enforce his rights to a written statement).

Occupational Sick Pay Schemes

8.6   Obviously if there is a scheme operated by the company it becomes even more important for that scheme's terms and conditions to be

---

[1] [1982] I.R.L.R. 183.

clearly set out. Employees must understand what rates of pay they will obtain and over what period. For example will full salary be paid for a period of, say, one month and then half salary thereafter? Does the employer wish to retain generally a discretion as to how much salary will be paid during the period of absence over and above S.S.P.? What is the position if an employee is ill whilst on holiday; is it intended simply to use the already agreed qualifying days during the period of holiday or is only one day to count as a qualifying day? These are the sort of questions which an employer will have to deal with when setting up an occupational sick pay scheme and indeed may well be the sort of questions an employee will ask or, if there is a recognised union, the union may raise it with the employer.

In essence the Court of Appeal in *Mears* (see above) said that the parties or a tribunal should not make any presumption as to whether or not there is a non-statutory entitlement to sick pay but should look at the agreement to see what was agreed either expressly or implicitly. This may ultimately involve analysing the conduct of the parties to see if it evidenced what was agreed but was not written down.

Additional problems may arise. For example, is the employee entitled to full wages during the period of ill health or only part wages? Once again it is necessary to look at the contract or at the conduct of the parties to see what could reasonably have been inferred as being agreed between employer and employee.

8.7 Two other points should be noted regarding occupational sick pay schemes. First, if an employee has fully used up the entitlement to occupational sick pay it is not automatically fair to dismiss the employee. The usual tests as to whether a dismissal was fair will apply.

Secondly, it would appear that the existence of a scheme does not mean that the employee must be retained until the entitlement has been used up before the employer can consider dismissing the employee. In most cases the scheme deals only with an entitlement to payment, not with an entitlement to be retained by the employer, see the Industrial Tribunal's decision in *Coulson v. Felixstowe Dock Company*.[2]

Disciplinary Action

8.8 Clarity is additionally important because of the possibility of disciplinary action being taken against an employee who has lengthy periods of

---

[2] [1975] I.R.L.R. 11.

absence. An employer may well be considering disciplinary action and if the company rules on ill health are clearly set out then there is less likely to be disagreement over what action the company can take.

State Sickness Benefit

8.9 State sickness benefit is payable providing an employee has paid the necessary number of contributions into a National Insurance Scheme. In most cases however it cannot be claimed until there have been 28 weeks of sickness when an employee will normally transfer from S.S.P. to state sickness benefit.

Statutory Sick Pay

8.10 On April 6, 1983, all employers became liable to pay employees' S.S.P. at the appropriate rate up to the equivalent of 28 weeks. There is a limit now on payment for a maximum of three years. Section 26 of the Social Security and Housing Benefit Act 1982 provides a definition of an employee which is substantially different to that provided by E.P.C.A. but in turn the 1982 Act is amended by various regulations which merely complicate matters. In most cases an employer should have little difficulty in deciding who is an employee.

Excluded Classes

8.11 There are various excluded categories of employees who are not entitled to claim S.S.P. at all. The time for determining whether an employee is a member of an excluded class or not is at the beginning of the illness or disability. If they are excluded because they fall into one of those categories they then must look to state sickness benefits instead.

The Social Security and Housing Benefits Act 1982, Schedule 1 sets out the excluded classes and they include, *inter alia*:

(a) pensioners;
(b) short-term employees, *i.e.* those who had a contract for a specified period of three months or less;
(c) low-paid employees, *i.e.* those who have not earned enough to attract National Insurance Contributions;
(d) strikers, that is where on the relevant day there was a stoppage of work due to a trade dispute at his workplace unless the employee had not participated in the dispute or had no direct interest in its outcome;
(e) pregnant employees, *i.e.* a woman who is still serving out her period of disqualification on account of pregnancy. The disqualification period is from 11 weeks before the expected week of confinement until six weeks after it.

Qualifying for S.S.P.

8.12 Three conditions must be met for an employee to qualify for S.S.P.:

(a) the day of absence must form part of a period of incapacity for work ('P.I.W.');
(b) the day of absence must be part of a period of entitlement;
(c) the day of absence must be a qualifying day.

Period of Incapacity for Work—P.I.W.

8.13 (a) A P.I.W. is a period of four or more consecutive days each of which is a day when the employee is (or is deemed to be) unfit for work because of physical or mental illness or disablement.[3] If

---

[3] S.2(2) of the 1982 Act.

the employee is not able to perform his normal task or the whole of his normal tasks but can do other duties within his contract then he does not qualify for S.S.P. as he is capable of work. Special rules apply to night-shift workers where the shift spans midnight.

(b) It is possible to 'link' two P.I.W.s providing they are not separated by more than eight weeks. If they are not then they count as one P.I.W. but in order to be considered as a P.I.W. it is necessary that each period must be of at least four consecutive qualifying days' duration. The advantage to the employee is that the usual rules regarding 'waiting days' (see below) will not apply.

Period of Entitlement

The period of entitlement is a period beginning with the start of a P.I.W. and ending with whichever of the following occurs first:

(a) the employee is fit for work;
(b) the employee has exhausted his entitlement to S.S.P.;
(c) a pregnant employee has reached the disqualifying period;
(d) the employee's contract with the employer concerned is ended.

Qualifying Days

8.14   (a) It must be appreciated that an employee who is ill for four consecutive days is not automatically entitled to S.S.P. The days must count as qualifying days. These are days of the week on which the employer and employee are agreed that the employee would normally be required to work under his contract of employment or days which are chosen to reflect the normal pattern of working.

(b) In the absence of any agreement the general regulations provide that the qualifying days will be the day or days on which it is agreed the employee would be required to work or, where it is agreed there are no such days, the Wednesday. There is complete flexibility for employers and employees to reach agreement as to qualifying days but under the legislation there must be at least one qualifying day. The aim of the legislation is to avoid a period of illness whereby the employer and employee then agree that those days amount to qualifying days; therefore, the qualifying days should be agreed beforehand.

(c) For an employee on the normal five-day working week the qualifying days would generally be Monday to Friday but it is open to employers to agree that all days of the week should qualify.

(d) Qualifying days are additionally important because the specified weekly rate is divided by the number of qualifying days in a week.

Waiting Days

The first three days in a P.I.W. are described as 'waiting days' and **8.15** S.S.P. is not payable. Under the contract of employment an employee may be paid but the employer is not entitled to deduct such payments from the National Insurance Contributions. Where there is a linked P.I.W. and there have already been waiting days served, then the employee will not have to serve any more waiting days.

Payment of S.S.P.

S.S.P. due to an employee should be paid on the first normal pay day **8.16** after a P.I.W. has been established or if that is impractical the next normal pay day. The payment cannot be made in kind but otherwise an employer may choose whatever method of payment he wishes and furthermore S.S.P. can be set off against any contractual entitlement.

The employee is not entitled to double payment. So he cannot receive payment under the company's occupational scheme and S.S.P. If he is entitled to S.S.P. that is taken into account when making the contractual payment but, for example where there are waiting days being served, the employer should bear in mind that he cannot reclaim any contractual payments made in respect of days where S.S.P. is not payable.

Notifying Sickness Absence

In order for consideration to be given as to whether or not an **8.17** employee is entitled to S.S.P. the employee must notify the employer that he is sick. Remember this does not necessarily mean that this is evidence of incapacity. Under Regulation 13 of the General Regulations (see above) an employer is entitled to make clear to the employee how he wants notification to be given, for example by telephone or in writing or indeed both.

The employer cannot require notification earlier than the first qualifying day of sickness nor indeed can he specify the time of day but notification in writing is treated as being given on the day that such notification was posted.

Notification can be made by someone else on the employee's behalf but the employer cannot require notification in the form of medical evidence although such medical evidence will count as notification.

There is nothing to stop the employer imposing stricter notification rules particularly where the employer has an occupational scheme. However it must be borne in mind that if there is a dispute as to whether or not late notification has been given and the late notification complies with S.S.P. but not the company rules then S.S.P. is payable.

If there has been late notification, that is late notification under the S.S.P. rules, and the employer is satisfied that there was no good cause for the lateness (good cause is not defined) the employer may withhold S.S.P. for the same number of qualifying days. Days where S.S.P. is withheld because of late notification do not count towards liability to pay S.S.P. for 28 weeks.

Evidence of Incapacity

8.18   There is no statutory requirement of evidence of incapacity although most employers will use well-established methods of self certification with medical certificates being required for more than seven days' absence.

The Contractual Position and Occuptional Sick Pay Schemes

8.19   In respect of all matters which arise under S.S.P. it is open to the employer in any occupational scheme to enhance the terms and conditions. The employer may even be prepared to extend the definition of an employee for the purposes of sick pay thereby including those who are excluded classes as set out in paragraph 3.3 above.

General Points

It is all very well for the employer to be able to withhold S.S.P. for the **8.20** period of late notification as set out in paragraph 8.28 above. For the employer, however, there is the more serious consideration of needing to reorganise the work as a result of the employee's absence. Notification by a certain time may be particularly important so whilst there is the sanction of withholding pay if there are continued absences with inadequate notification the employer may well wish to consider instituting disciplinary proceedings.

The employer may also wish to receive satisfactory evidence of incapacity. There is little he can do for the first seven days. Obviously if there are continual absences for short periods an employer may wish to reserve the right to seek a medical report from the employee's general practitioner (subject to the Access to Medical Reports Act 1988). Alternatively the employer may wish to have the company's doctor examine the employee. The employer also needs to decide whether or not a report or certificate from, for example, chiropractor or osteopath will be acceptable evidence and so far as it is possible any policy should be set out in writing.

There are duties upon the employer to give the employee written **8.21** reasons why they are not being paid S.S.P. An employer may wish to consider incorporating this aspect of a dispute into the grievance procedure before being required to give written reasons.

Whether it is practical to incorporate terms relating to sick pay into a contract of employment is debatable. This may be one of those matters which should properly be dealt with either in a separate document or, if there is one, a staff manual or handbook. Appendix 8 lists those points which should be borne in mind when drafting a contract.

CHAPTER 9

TRANSFER OF UNDERTAKINGS

Introduction

The Transfer of Undertakings (Protection of Employment) Regulations **9.1**
1981 (S.I. 1981, No. 1794) (see Appendix 9), were approved by
Parliament pursuant to the European Communities Act 1972 and in an
attempt to implement Council Directive 77/187/EEC. They came into
effect during 1982 and applied to situations where someone transfers a
commercial undertaking or a part thereof to another person. They
provide that such a transfer will not operate to terminate employees'
contracts of employment but that any contract which would have been
terminated by the transfer will continue as if made between the
transferee and the employee. Some would say this is enforced slavery
since there are many situations in which an employee would not
necessarily want to go with a business that is being transferred to a new
owner. Be that as it may the provisions of the regulations largely
supplant the provisions of section 94 of E.P.C.A. That section dealt with
what happens in circumstances where there is a change of ownership
of a business. Subsection (2) provided that if, by agreement with the
employee, the new owner renews the employee's contract of employment or re-engages the employee under a new contract of employment
then sections 84 and 90 of E.P.C.A. which deal with the exclusions of
rights to redundancy payments in certain circumstances are deemed to
apply just as if the employment had been renewed by the previous
owner of the business. The effect of the interaction of
the sections is that there is deemed to be no dismissal by reason of the
ending of the employment under the previous contract with the previous
owner of the business.

Regulation 3—A Relevant Transfer

9.2   The regulations apply to a transfer from one person to another of 'an undertaking' situated immediately before the transfer in the United Kingdom or part of an undertaking which is situated in the United Kingdom. A transfer of an undertaking or a part can be carried out by a series of two or more transactions as to which see below.

Transfers by Receivers, Liquidators and Administrators

9.3   There are special provisions relating to receivers, liquidators or administrators of a company appointed under Part 2 of the Insolvency Act 1986. Where such a person transfers the company's business to a wholly owned subsidiary, that is to say a 'hive down,' then such a transfer shall not be deemed to have been effected until either the hive down company ceases to be a wholly owned subsidiary of the transferor or the business is transferred by the hive down company to someone else. This is to avoid the transfer taking effect for the purposes of the regulations until the hive down company has been sold off.

The Effect of Transfers on Contracts of Employment— Regulation 5

9.4   A relevant transfer, that is to say one referred to above, shall not operate so as to terminate the contract of employment of any person employed by the transferor company *in the business or part transferred.* Any such contract of employment which would otherwise have been terminated by the transfer shall have effect after the transfer as if originally made between the employee and the transferee company. This means simply that if employees are employed by a transferor company in the business being transferred then the contract 'goes over' to the acquiring company. All the transferor's rights, powers and liabilities go over but this only affects employees who were employed in the business 'immediately before the transfer'. There has been considerable case law on what that means (see paragraph 9.13 below).

The Effect of Relevant Transfers on Collective Agreements—Regulation 6 and Regulation 9

Where at the time of a transfer there exists a collective agreement **9.5** with a trade union recognised by the transferor in respect of employees whose contracts are preserved by the regulations, the agreement also 'goes over.' There will therefore be recognition by operation of law on the part of the transferee company and this is clearly something that vendors and purchasers of companies and businesses need to think about quite carefully.

Pensions—Regulation 7

Occupational pension schemes are not affected. There has been **9.6** much discussion about the position of pensions in circumstances where companies are sold and the Hanson exercise in relation to Courage received a great deal of publicity. The Occupational Pensions Board has reported with recommendations to avoid the rape of corporate pension schemes in take-overs. As to this see below in the section on pensions. (Chap. 10 para. 10.27).

Dismissals Because of Transfers—Regulation 8

An employee is regarded as unfairly dismissed when the reason is **9.7** connected with a transfer, whether the dismissal occurs before or after the transfer. However when the reason is an economic, technical or organisational one involving changes in the workforce of either the transferor or transferee, before or after a relevant transfer, then there is a substantial reason justifying dismissal. There has been case law which indicates that a request by a purchaser of a business for the vendor to dismiss certain people before the transfer so as to avoid the purchaser having to take on those employees is not a dismissal for an economical, technical or organisational reason and is therefore prima facie unfair.

Information and Consultation of
Trade Unions—Regulation 10

9.8 There are obligations upon employers to inform and consult recognised trade unions long enough before the transfer to enable consultation to take place. The obligation is to inform the union:

(a) that the relevant transfer is to take place;
(b) when it is to take place and the reasons for it;
(c) the legal, economic and social implications of the transfer for affected employees;
(d) the measures which are envisaged which will be taken in connection with the transfer in relation to the employees and if there are no measures, that fact;
(e) if the employer is the transferor the measures which the transferee envisages he will take.

The failure to comply with these obligations gives rise to a right to make a claim to an Industrial Tribunal. In *National Association of Theatrical Television and Kine Employees* v. *Rank Leisure Ltd.*,[1] it was held by a majority that the duty to consult only arises if the employer of affected employees envisages taking 'measures' in relation to them. 'Measures' must mean measures in addition to the actual transfer and since there were no such measures in the particular case there was no obligation to *consult*. However, while the Area Officer knew what was going on, it was not sufficient for a union representative to pick up information informally in this way. He must be *notified* properly in accordance with the regulations. The duty to inform only arises where there is a binding agreement to a transfer or it is otherwise clear that the transfer will take place. The speed with which the transaction had to be completed was a 'special' circumstance under regulation 10. Nevertheless, in view of the urgency, Rank should have written to the union by the day after the signing of the contract at the latest and they could have had the letter delivered instead of posting it. These were steps which were reasonably practicable and because Rank had not taken them there had been a failure to inform the trade union representatives in respect of all employees for whom the union was recognised. Any

---

[1] (Unreported: I.T. 1388/134).

loss suffered as a result of the failure to inform was however very small, if not negligible, since they continued in the same jobs with the same contractual rights and they had in any case known of the possibility of the transfer since September 3. No compensation was awarded.

Regulation 10(7) provides that if in any case there are special **9.9** circumstances which render it not reasonably practicable for an employer to perform a duty imposed upon him by the regulations, he shall take all such steps towards performing that duty as are reasonably practicable in the circumstances. The facts were that, during September 1982, Rank carried on negotiations with E for the sale of a West End cinema as a going concern. E was to take over all the staff. The staff were told on September 3 that negotiations were in progress and the area officer knew. E was anxious to complete by October 3 and the agreement for sale was signed on September 27 after a weekend of negotiations. The staff were given a statement on September 29 and Rank's operations executive explained matters to them at a meeting on that day at which the area officer was present. The staff were told that their contracts would be automatically transferred under the regulations and that the terms and conditions would be identical except for pension rights. On the same day Rank's personnel executive wrote to the area officer giving him the same information, although the letter was not received until October 4. The transfer took place from the close of business on October 2 and on October 6 the union presented an originating application.

The regulations do not say in what form information must be conveyed **9.10** to the union and the tribunal thought that on balance the regulations require the information to be in writing. Note that the duty to *inform* covers a situation where the employer envisages that no measures will be taken in relation to the affected employees but the duty to *consult* arises only when the employer of affected employees does envisage taking measures in relation to them.

The regulations were further watered down, however, by *Institution of* **9.11** *Professional Civil Servants and Others* v. *Secretary of State for Defence*,[2] in which it was held by Mr. Justice Millett in the Chancery Division that the duty to *inform* recognised trade unions about measures only arises where a definite plan or proposal is in prospect for implementation. The Dockyard Services Act 1986 was passed to facilitate the transfer to commercial management of the dockyards at Rosyth and Devonport in early 1987. The employees would be transferred from the civil service to the private companies. The Act required the Secretary of State to give certain information about the transfer to

---

[2] [1987] I.R.L.R. 373.

the unions and to enter into consultations. The relevant parts of the Act in fact re-enacted regulation 10 of the Transfer Regulations without any material changes. It was held that the duty to inform unions arises when the company has formulated a definite plan or proposal and that the words 'long enough before the transfer to enable consultation to take place' mean 'as soon as measures are envisaged and, if possible, long enough before the transfer.' It was recognised that there are developing situations and it may be that particular measures will not be envisaged until shortly before the transfers. It is not enough that the company has some mere possibility in contemplation, furthermore, the words 'in connection with the transfer' must mean on or after and as a result of the transfer—the connection is both temporal and causal.

9.12 Finally, the unions were not entitled to dictate the form in which the information to which they were entitled was provided. The Secretary of State was well within his rights when extracting the required information from the actual documents and supplying that information while withholding the documents himself.

'Immediately Before'

9.13 There are two areas of substantial controversy in relation to the regulations, first the definition of 'immediately before' in relation to whether or not employees are covered by the regulations because they are employed in the business 'immediately before the transfer.' In *Secretary of State* v. *Spence*[3] the Court of Appeal held that employees dismissed by the transferor three hours before the transfer were not covered by the regulations and they were entitled to a redundancy payment from the vendor. This was consistent with the European Court of Justice in *Wendelboe* v. *L.J. Music (No. 19/83)*[4] and *Mikkelsen* v. *Danmols Inventar A/S (No. 105/84)*.[5] In *Brook Lane Finance* v. *Bradley*[6] the E.A.T. pointed out that *Spence* conflicted with the *obiter* from the Court of Appeal in *Teeside Times Ltd.* v. *Drury*[7] and leave to appeal to the Court of Appeal was given to decide whether *Spence* was incorrectly decided. The matter may have been put beyond doubt by the House of Lords in *Litster* v. *Forth Dry Dock & Engineering Co. Ltd.*,[8] in

---

[3] [1986] I.R.L.R. 248.
[4] [1985] E.C.R. 457.
[5] [1986] 1 C.M.L.R. 316.
[6] [1988] I.R.L.R. 283.
[7] [1980] I.R.L.R. 72.
[8] [1989] I.R.L.R. 161.

which Lord Oliver held that although as a matter of language when employees were dismissed one hour before the transfer, they were not employed immediately before the transfer, the purpose of the EEC Directive and the regulations was to safeguard rights of employees on a transfer and that it was permissible to read in to the regulation the words 'or would have been so employed if he had not been unfairly dismissed in the circumstances described in regulation 8(1)' after 'immediately before.' The reason for the dismissal was the transfer and although they were not employed immediately before the transfer, in his view their employment continued with the transferee. The House of Lords was unanimous. It seems that *Litster* may be distinguishable on its facts and that *Spence* may not have been wholly reversed. There is, it is regretted, more legal controversy to follow.

Automatic Unfair Dismissal

9.14 The second area of controversy arises under regulation 8 which provides that if an employee is dismissed by reason of the transfer then the dismissal is automatically unfair unless it is for an economic, technical or organisational reason. It is unclear whether insistence by the purchaser that employees be dismissed comes within the definition of economic. In *Wheeler* v. *Patel*[9] it was held that economic had to be construed with technical and organisational as relating to the conduct of the business itself, therefore the desire to obtain the best price could not be 'economic.' This approach was followed by the E.A.T. in *Gateway Hotels* v. *Stewart*[10] being preferred over that adopted in the Scottish case of *Anderson* v. *Dalkeith Engineering Ltd.*[11] In *Wheeler* it was held that if the reason for dismissal was no more than a desire to obtain an enhanced price, or no more than a desire to achieve a sale, it was not an economic reason for the purposes of regulation 8 and in *Gateway Hotels* it was said that it was clear that the respondents were dismissed simply in order not to lose the sale, therefore the employers failed to show that the respondents were dismissed for an economic reason connected with the meaning of the business within the meaning of regulation 8 and the dismissals were therefore unfair.

---

[9] [1987] I.C.R. 631.
[10] [1988] I.R.L.R. 287.
[11] [1984] I.R.L.R. 429.

CHAPTER **10**

PENSIONS—THE CONTRACTUAL POSITION

Introduction

The contract of employment could include specific contractual pension **10.1**
promises enforceable directly against the employer. If all contracts
were so drafted, this would be a very short chapter. Such contracts are
however very much the exception, usually being the price of securing
the services of key employees. They can and do sometimes arise by
accident, as a result of unthinking oral representations.

Prior to April 6, 1988, it was possible for membership of the **10.2**
employer's pension scheme to be compulsory as a condition of
employment, but the norm in contracts made since that date has been
to refer to the existence of a pension scheme run by the employer and
the terms on which the employee might join. This satisfies the minimum
requirements of section 1 of E.P.C.A. but is of little help in determining
whether the benefits under the scheme are contractual.

Complications arise where there is a specific pension promise by **10.3**
reference to a particular pension scheme. Are the pension scheme's
documents incorporated into the contract of employment and what is
the effect of the pension scheme clause stating that nothing in the
pension scheme deed shall affect the contract of employment? This
question does not appear to have been litigated.

The law relating to the enforceability of pension rights and expecta- **10.4**
tions is in a state of flux. Despite various judicial decisions over the past
50 years, a number of statutes which bear on the subject and even the
advent of EEC law, the legal nature of pension rights remains uncertain.
From a theoretical standpoint, the crux of the matter is whether a
pension is deferred pay, an implied term of an employee's contract of
employment or merely a gratuitous promise on the part of the employer.

In real life, practical considerations, and particularly those of an industrial relations nature, are all important.

The Historical Development of Pension Schemes

10.5   The earliest pensions were granted to faithful retainers as a reward for long service. Each payment by the employer was gratuitous, and the payment of further instalments could not be enforced. Gradually such arrangements came to be funded in advance, but there was still no right to receive a pension, unless the retainer stayed in service until the required retirement age.

10.6   Advance funding did nevertheless bring protection for the potential pensioner, because such funding was placed in trust, safe from the employer's creditors. Today, when the vast majority of United Kingdom occupational pension schemes are funded in advance, trust law, not contract, remains the lynchpin. Whilst this provides security for the scheme's beneficiaries to the extent of the assets already held in trust, it gives those beneficiaries enforceable rights only against the scheme's trustees, and adds nothing to their direct contractual rights against the employer. (It is nevertheless a fact that claims for loss of pension rights in unfair dismissal claims are made against the employer rather than against the trustees.)

Beneficiaries Rights Against Trustees of a Pension Fund

10.7   The beneficiaries' enforceable rights against the trustees are limited to those benefits which they enjoy as of right under the scheme's provisions. To maintain an acceptable degree of flexibility, trustees are usually given wide discretions to grant additional benefits. They cannot be forced to exercise those discretions. Nor, insofar as they do exercise any discretion, can the manner of the exercise (in the absence of mala fides) be reviewed by the Court. Beneficiaries' rights are however being steadily increased by interventionist legislation, for example in the areas of benefits on leaving service before normal pensionable age and of disclosure of information about the scheme.

The Tax Position

Funded pension schemes have to date invariably been designed to **10.8** be 'exempt approved schemes' under Chapter I, Part XIV of the Income and Corporation Taxes Act 1988, in order to obtain both for the employer and the employees all the tax advantages of such status.

The present Government is however set on the path of 'fiscal **10.9** neutrality,' which in simple terms would impose much lower general rates of tax in return for, *inter alia*, the reduction in the tax breaks enjoyed by pension schemes. The then Chancellor embarked on this course in 1986 with legislation designed to curb excess scheme 'surpluses,' continued it in 1987 with benefit limits aimed at the higher paid (those earning over £100,000) and took a considerable further stride in the 1989 Budget, so that, in general terms, for new members of existing schemes after June 1, 1989, and members of new schemes, only pension benefits based on a salary of a maximum of £60,000 will be eligible for tax relief. This figure is presently to be index-linked by reference to prices and not salaries, with the result that, according to actuaries, it will in 30 years' time be halved in real terms. Top-up unapproved schemes enjoying no tax reliefs, other than a corporation tax deduction for the employer, will be expected to fill the gaps, and with the passage of time they will clearly become of great importance.

One of the main requirements of an exempt approved scheme is the **10.10** irrevocable declaration of a trust, the trust being declared by the employer (as *de facto* settlor). Separate trustees are usually appointed.

The Interim Trust Deed

The legal documents necessary to obtain full exempt approved status **10.11** commonly present a forbidding aspect to the layman in their length and complexity. Nowadays the major causes are legislative requirements, but since the provision of company pensions is officially encouraged, the Superannuation Funds Office ('S.F.O.') of the Inland Revenue (which polices exempt approved schemes) will allow temporary tax reliefs to the members of a new scheme on the strength solely of an Interim Trust Deed, which (*inter alia*) declares irrevocable trusts, confirms that the new scheme will be operated in accordance with all relevant statutory requirements, and promises that a further deed containing all the necessary details will be executed within two years (or such longer period as the S.F.O. may allow). This further deed is known as the Definitive Trust Deed.

The Definitive Trust Deed

10.12 For historical reasons, the Definitive Trust Deed is usually split into two parts: the Deed itself, containing the trusts and powers, and the Rules, containing the benefit provisions. Only when the entire Definitive Trust Deed and Rules has been blessed by the S.F.O. does a scheme achieve full exempt approved status.

10.13 The Definitive Trust Deed and Rules are usually comprehensible only to those involved in pensions, although under the statutory disclosure regulations, they must be available to beneficiaries, both actual and potential (meaning members, their spouses and their dependants). The disclosure legislation also details the basic information about a scheme that must be given, and such information is usually incorporated in a booklet. In practice, the booklet is all that the average member sees.

Contractual Effect of the Definitive Trust Deed

10.14 What contractual effect do the Definitive Trust Deed and Rules and the booklet have? Most of the cases on the point starting with that of *Ward* v. *Barclay Perkins & Co. Ltd.*,[1] appear to conclude that the pension scheme does form part of the contract of employment. One recent case, *Duke* v. *Reliance Systems Ltd.*,[2] however appears to have decided the contrary, as the employer's general retirement policy (under which women retired at 60) was held to override the provisions of the pension scheme (under which there was a common retirement age of 65). In a very recent case[3] it was held that the employer held out it's scheme as a valuable part of the package and it was implicit in the contract of employment that the employer agreed with the employee it would duly discharge its pension fund functions in good faith. On the facts it did.

---

[1] [1939] 1 All E.R. 287.
[2] [1988] I.C.R. 449.
[3] *Milhenstedt* v. *Barclays Bank p.l.c., The Times* July 28 1989, C.A.

CONTRACTUAL EFFECT OF THE DEFINITIVE TRUST DEED

On the assumption that the pension scheme does form part of the **10.15** contract of employment, what is the effect of the various clauses that the pension lawyer acting for an employer will invariably recommend? Such clauses will:

(a) give the employer, more often with the consent of the trustees, power to amend the provisions of the scheme. (It is not uncommon nowadays for this power to be totally unqualified);

(b) allow the employer to reduce, suspend or terminate its contributions; and

(c) give the employer power to cause the termination of the scheme in certain circumstances.

If appropriately drafted, these powers will be beneficial powers in the hands of the employer, and he will be able to exercise them without the consent of the members. That is not to say that in so doing the employer will not be in breach of the members' contracts of employment, under which the members have direct privity with their employer. The scheme trustees will also have a duty (under trust law, not contract law) to protect their members' best interests, insofar as their powers extend.

In practice, the employer's powers to reduce, suspend or terminate **10.16** contributions or to terminate the scheme will not normally be fettered by specific contractual promises to members. Furthermore, because such actions by their nature restrict or terminate the accrual of *future* benefits, benefits earned in respect of *past* service will (in simplistic terms) be unaffected.

The Power to Amend the Terms of a Pension Scheme

It is the power to amend which must be exercised with caution, in **10.17** case an amendment which reduces or restricts members' rights or benefits leads to claims for constructive (and unfair) dismissal. To reduce such a risk to a minimum, employment lawyers now often seek to include in the contract of employment advance acceptance on the part of the employee of the employer's right to amend the terms of the pension scheme. How effective such an acceptance is in the eyes of the Court remains to be seen. The fact that membership of pension schemes can no longer be made compulsory, but is entirely optional, must lend weight to the employer's case.

If an employer wishes to amend his scheme to the detriment of the **10.18** members and without their consent, but at the same time to avoid successful claims for breach of contract, he is likely to have to demonstrate that in all the circumstances the amendments are reasonable—the ultimate distinction being between a job with a pension and a job without. What is reasonable will be different in each case and depend on the nature and materiality of the changes. Thus an amendment to a scheme's early retirement provisions might be considered reasonable, whereas a change of the normal retiring age might well not be. The case of *B.P. Chemicals* v. *Joseph*[4] concerned a change of normal retiring age from 65 to 60. The Employment Appeal Tribunal held that where there is a question as to whether an employee's normal retiring age (as opposed to pensionable age) has been changed, what has to be asked is whether the contractual position between the parties has been altered. Usually, that will involve an inquiry as to whether the employee has understood the change and consented to it. If it is clear that there has been a change in the contractual relationship, then the normal retiring age may be changed. In this case, the change in Mr. Joseph's terms of employment was being made by the change in his pension scheme. It was sufficiently fundamental that his employer had a strict legal obligation to make this clear to him. (In fact the Tribunal held that B.P. had fulfilled this obligation.)

10.19 The need to obtain members' consent to changes will usually be capable of practical resolution. If the employer has good reasons for wishing to make the changes and has the ultimate threat of being able to terminate the scheme, members will probably prefer to accept the changes on the best terms they can negotiate, rather than see their scheme lapse. They will also have the protection of the trustees, whose consent to amendments will probably be necessary, and who must act in the best interests of their beneficiaries. In practice though, the trustees may also be shareholders in, or members of the management of, the employer, and thus have conflicts of interest, which they find difficulty in putting behind them.

Schemes Contracted Out of the State Earnings Related Pensions Scheme

10.20 Section 50 of the Social Security Pensions Act 1975 must also be borne in mind. Where a scheme is contracted-out of the State Earnings Related Pensions Scheme, certain amendments to it will only be valid once approved by the Occupational Pensions Board ('O.P.B.'). Follow-

---

[4] [1980] I.R.L.R. 55.

ing the considerable dilution of section 50 made by the Social Security Act 1986, the O.P.B.'s consent to rule changes is now needed only in respect of rules dealing with eligibility for membership and all aspects of guaranteed minimum pensions.

Position on the Sale of a Company

Another situation where the rights of pension scheme members come **10.21** into sharp focus is when the company or business for which they work is sold and they have to leave the Group scheme of which they have been members. Even though the agreement effecting the sale and purchase may contain very detailed pension provisions, the members are not parties thereto; nor are the trustees of the schemes which they are leaving or being invited to join. The members' rights on the enforced termination of their membership are often only to the minimum leaving service benefits, and what they are offered by way of past and future service benefits in their new scheme will depend on many factors related mainly to the economic strengths, or otherwise, of the vendor, the purchaser and the vendor's scheme and on which the members can have no influence.

Future Trends

So what of the future? More interventionist legislation seems likely, but **10.22** not to change the legal basis of pension schemes.

Paragraph 4.12 of the February 1989 report of the O.P.B. says: **10.23**

> "We believe that . . . it is not clear from a legal standpoint whether the prospective benefits, which an employee might receive from his pension scheme, give him a contractual right against the employer. Our report has been prepared on the assumption that the employees' pension rights and expectations are essentially a matter between them and the trustees, but the question has fundamental implications. For example, if an employer exercises a right to wind up a scheme, the beneficiaries have to rely under present law on the assets in the trust; there is no claim against the employer."

The report then refers to the recommendation in the O.P.B.'s 1982 report that the matter should be investigated, and adds that the issue remains unresolved, but that it is outside the scope of the present report.

(Examples of expectations are discretionary increases to pensions in payment and benefits on a winding-up augmented beyond the minimum leaving service benefits.)

10.24 The report does nevertheless make some recommendations which bear on the issues raised in this Chapter.

10.25 Whilst in paragraph 8.15 of the report the O.P.B. recommends that "trust law should continue as the legal basis of pension schemes," paragraph 8.16 says that:

> " . . . in our view it would be desirable for an authority other than the High Court—possibly the pensions tribunal recommended in Chapter 13—to have a general power to amend all types of pension scheme, whether occupational or personal. In occupational schemes such amendment should be subject to consultation with the beneficiaries or their representatives and possibly other safeguards. In particular it should be possible to amend a scheme where winding-up has commenced or where an employer, who had the power to amend or to consent to amendment, no longer exists."

Paragraph 8.17 contains the recommendation that "a simplified procedure should be established for the amendment of all types of pension arrangement." If such a procedure is introduced, care will have to be used in its exercise to ensure that contractual rights are not thereby defeated.

10.26 Chapter 10 deals with the winding-up of a scheme on its termination. Paragraph 10.11 recommends that, when the termination occurs as a result of the insolvency of the employer, there should be overriding legislation to prescribe minimum winding-up benefits for members. Paragraph 10.17 recommends the same requirement where a scheme is wound up, and the employer and the employments continue undisturbed.

10.27 Chapter 11 discusses the security of members' benefits in payment, following the takeover or insolvency of the employer. Paragraph 11.4 reads:

> "An argument in favour of a discretionary framework is that an employer does not have to establish a pension scheme and those who do so should be free as far as possible to settle its terms. In particular, employers, having accepted the essentially unpredictable cost of a final pay scheme, wish to keep maximum room for manoeuvre on future costs, and they may well be content for substantial pension increases to be provided from scheme resources, or sometimes at their own cost, provided that this does not establish an obligation for further increases to be granted in future. Any move to require pension increases to be guaranteed might work against the members' interests because employers would want a more conservative policy to be followed or might indeed decide to discontinue their final pay schemes altogether."

Paragraph 11.5 goes on:

"A retiring employee, on the other hand, will probably wish his pension to be based on final pay and also needs to know where he stands financially not only at the point of retirement but also thereafter. Ideally he needs assurance as to the extent that his pension will be adjusted to take account of inflation."

Then in paragraph 11.28 the O.P.B. recommends that:

"Employers and trustees should be urged as a matter of good practice to guarantee, on pensions in payment other than G.M.P.s, increases at least equal to price-indexing up to 5 per cent. a year. The guarantee should preferably apply to all scheme members, but should at least cover all current pensioners. Schemes that do not guarantee increases at least up to 5 per cent. a year to all current pensioners should offer those not covered by a guarantee the pensioners' option '[to take a lower initial pension increased subsequently at a fixed rate, the proposed details of which are]' outlined in paragraphs 11.19 to 11.21."

The Government has accepted the Board's rcommendations and has **10.28** presented the report as a White Paper; what legislation will follow remains to be seen.

EEC Law and the Future of Pensions Law

European Community law is also in the minds of pension practitioners, **10.29** in the area of equal treatment of the sexes for pension purposes. Occupational pension schemes are for the time being able to provide different normal pension ages for men and women, and this is likely to continue whilst the State maintains different State pension ages for men and women. The EEC is, however, intent on the equalisation of state pension ages and occupational pension schemes will, when that occurs, also have to fall in line. A significant case in this area, *Clarke* v. *Cray Precision Engineering Ltd.*[5] was in May 1989 referred direct to the European Court of Justice by the President of the E.A.T. without any formal judgment on the merits of the case. At first instance the industrial tribunal held that the benefits provided by the company's contracted-out contributory pension scheme are 'pay' within the meaning of Article 119, payment to the applicant, a man, at the age of 60, of a pension less

---

[5] C.O.I.T. 14229/87.

than that payable to a woman is discrimination and that the applicant could rely on Article 199 to obtain a remedy against the respondent. See paragraph 11.9 below for further comment.

10.30 Schedule 3 of the Social Security Bill 1989 (which the Government is obliged to introduce to comply with EC Directive 86/378) will when it comes into force (presumably on January 1, 1993), require that every 'employment related benefit scheme' complies with the principle of equal treatment for men and women (with the notable exception of normal pension ages referred to above). In practical terms, the greatest effect of the Schedule is likely to be that part-time employees (the majority of whom are women) will have to be offered membership of their employer's pension scheme. To maintain their exclusion the employer would have to establish that it was based on objectively justified factors, unrelated to any discrimination on grounds of sex. Pension lawyers believe that such factors could include the test of the extent to which it is reasonable for the employer to have to make pension provision for his part-time employees on the same basis as for his full-time employees. The test may well be by reference to the number of hours worked, and commentators have suggested that employees working less than 16 hours will not benefit from the proposed legislation. Time will tell.

CHAPTER 11

EEC LEGISLATION

Introduction

The Treaty of Rome, being an international treaty, is not 'self-executing.' It **11.1** is a principle of United Kingdom constitutional law that international treaties do not execute themselves for domestic purposes and it was for that reason that Parliament had to pass the European Communities Act in 1972, which Act provides the legal foundation for the recognition of community law in the United Kingdom. United Kingdom sovereignty was preserved in one crucial respect. The 1972 Act is capable of amendment or appeal according to the will of any successive Parliament. The whole question of the interrelation between community law and United Kingdom law is, however, complicated further by the fact that section 2 of the European Communities Act does not provide for the automatic incorporation into United Kingdom law of all community law. Only such community provisions as are 'directly effective' under EEC law will become part of United Kingdom law without further enactment. The European Court of Justice has dealt with the question of direct effect in the Dutch case of *Van Gend en Loos*.[1] The Court there held that in order to be directly effective a provision must:

(a) confer individual rights;
(b) be clear and precise;
(c) be unconditional and unqualified.

These criteria have been applied both to certain articles in the Treaty **11.2** of Rome and to the various directives in deciding whether they can be

---

[1] [1963] C.M.L.R. 105.

enforced directly by individuals. If a provision of EEC law is directly effective, an individual can sue on it in national courts irrespective of whether or not that individual's own Member State has domestic or municipal laws which cover the point. Section 2(1) of the European Communities Act gives the statutory foundation:

" . . . all such rights, powers, liberties, obligations and restrictions from time to time created or arising by or under the treaties, and all such remedies and procedures from time to time provided for, by or under the treaties, as in accordance with the treaties are without further enactment to be given legal effect or used in the United Kingdom, shall be recognised and available in law and be enforced, allowed and followed accordingly."

Direct Applicability and Article 119

11.3 This question of direct applicability or direct effectiveness is enormously important for United Kingdom law in relation to contracts of employment mainly by reason of the provisions of Article 119 of the Treaty of Rome. That Article requires each Member State to establish and maintain the principle that men and women should receive equal pay for equal work. The Council of the EEC has power under the Treaty of Rome to issue directives to Member States which require the Member States to enact specific provisions designed to carry into effect the social and economic policies of the community. In the employment field, we have had the equal pay directive, the equal treatment directive, the social security directive and the directive on equal treatment in occupational social security schemes which must be implemented by Member States in 1993. Our own sex discrimination and equal pay law is largely derived from the principles contained within EEC directives and should, in theory, therefore, be fully harmonised with that of other Member States. In practice, however, there are fairly substantial discrepancies and questions as to the direct applicability of Article 119 have been raised on a number of occasions. It is of note that when the United Kingdom joined the EEC, the United Kingdom government was given an assurance by the EEC Commission that Article 119 would not have direct effect.

11.4 Notwithstanding this, the European Court of Justice held in the case of *Defrenne* v. *Sociètè Anoneme Belge de Navigation Aerienne*[2] that

---

[2] [1976] I.C.R. 547.

Article 119 was capable of direct application within all Member States, although only in respect of acts of 'direct and overt discrimination' identifiable by plain criteria of equal pay for equal work. In that case a Belgian air hostess claimed equal pay with a cabin steward who did the same work as her. The European Court of Justice held that Article 119 satisfied the criteria for direct effect set out in the *Van Gend en Loos* case (above) and it therefore established a fundamental principle of community law which could be enforced by individuals through their own national courts.

Definition of pay for purposes of Article 119

11.5 Since that time, the effect of Article 119 has been widened both by the extension of the definition of 'pay' and by extending its applicability to unlawful indirect discrimination as opposed to direct and overt.

11.6 For the purposes of the Article, pay is defined as:

> "the ordinary, basic or minimum wage or salary, and any other consideration, whether in cash or kind, which the worker receives, directly or indirectly, in respect of his employment from his employer."

11.7 In *Garland* v. *British Rail*,[3] travel concessions provided to the families of male employees only after their retirement, constituted pay under the Article since they were paid directly or indirectly in respect of employment. In *Hammersmith and Queen Charlotte's Special Health Authority* v. *Cato*[4] the E.A.T. held that a contractual redundancy payment is 'pay' for these purposes even though it is paid on termination of employment.

11.8 In the pensions field the type of scheme involved affects whether or not pension scheme contributions and benefits constitute pay. In *Worringham and Humphries* v. *Lloyds Bank Limited (No. 69/80)*[5] a distinction was drawn by the European Court between schemes which supplement the state social security scheme and schemes which are designed as a substitute for the whole or part of it. Substitutes are currently regarded as being outside the scope of Article 119. In

---

[3] [1983] 2 A.C. 751, (H.L.).
[4] [1987] I.R.L.R. 483.
[5] [1981] I.R.L.R. 178.

EEC LEGISLATION

Newstead v. *The Department of Transport*,[6] a contracted-out scheme which operated in complete substitution for the state scheme was held to be in reality a social security benefit and consequently outside the scope of Article 119. The position is slightly confused because in *Worringham* the European Court ruled that an employer's contributions to a contracted-out occupational pension scheme were 'pay' for the purposes of the Article and in *Bilka Kaufhaus GmbH* v. *Weber Von Hartz (No. 170/84)*[7] it was stated by the European Court that benefit payable under an occupational pension scheme which was based on an agreement between employer and employee and which supplemented the state scheme was covered by Article 119.

The Industrial Tribunal's Approach

11.9   The Industrial Tribunals have capitalised on the decision of the E.C.J. in the *Defrenne* case (see above) that Article 119 is directly applicable, and the subsequent broadening of the definition of 'pay' for the purposes of Article 119, to fill the gaps in United Kingdom legislation. A good example is the Tribunal decision in the case of *Clarke* v. *Cray Precision Engineering Ltd.*,[8] which, as indicated, has now been transferred by the E.A.T. to the European Court of Justice.

11.10   Mr. Clarke joined his employer's pension scheme when he began working for them in 1969. Pensionable ages under the scheme were 65 for men and 60 for women. If an employee chose to retire earlier than this, his or her pension was actuarially reduced. When Mr. Clarke decided to take early retirement at 60, his pension was reduced to about two-thirds of the pension that a female employee retiring at his age, on his salary, and with his length of service would have received. He complained to an Industrial Tribunal of sex discrimination, alleging a breach of Article 119.

11.11   The Tribunal considered, following *Worringham* and *Bilka-Kaufhaus*, that both the pension and the lump sum payable under the scheme of which Mr. Clarke was a member constituted 'pay' for the purposes of Article 119. If this is correct (and the decision is subject to appeal by the employers, now referred to the E.C.J.) it will have major implications for any occupational pension scheme which supplements, rather than

[6] [1986] I.R.L.R. 299, E.A.T.
[7] [1987] I.C.R. 110.
[8] C.O.I.T. 14229/87.

replaces, S.E.R.P.S. For example, the decision suggests that where such a scheme sets different pensionable ages for men and women and provides for the actuarial enhancement of the pension of a woman who works beyond her pensionable age, so that she receives more than a man of the same age and in the same circumstances, male colleagues could complain under Article 119. Similarly the decision indicates that there may be a breach of Article 119 where such a scheme applies different commutation factors when calculating lump sums for men and women, resulting in lump sums of different sizes.

As discussed earlier, the Sex Discrimination Act 1986 had no impact **11.12** on the discriminatory effect of the statutory redundancy scheme. In *Hammersmith and Queen Charlotte's Special Health Authority* v. *Cato* (see above at paragraph 11.7) the E.A.T. found that a contractual redundancy pay scheme which was based on the statutory scheme breached Article 119. In *Ogilvy-Stuart* v. *Cryer*[9] an Industrial Tribunal ruled that the statutory scheme is also in breach of Article 119. When Mrs. Ogilvy-Stuart was made redundant she had already passed her 60th birthday. Since section 82(1)(*b*) of E.P.C.A. stipulates that a woman is not entitled to a redundancy payment if she is aged 60 or over, Mrs. Ogilvy-Stuart's employers considered that they did not need to pay her a redundancy payment. She complained to an Industrial Tribunal that her employers had discriminated against her since a man of her age would have been paid a redundancy payment. She alleged that the statutory redundancy scheme was in breach of Article 119 and cited the E.A.T.'s decision in *Cato* in support.

Her employers argued that *Cato* was not applicable because there **11.13** the entitlement had been contractual. But the Tribunal did not accept that this was a valid distinction and concluded that the statutory scheme was in breach of Article 119 and that Mrs. Ogilvy-Stuart was entitled to compensation of an amount equal to the redundancy payment a comparable man would have received.

Two other Tribunal decisions have ruled that the statutory redundancy **11.14** scheme is in breach of Article 119—*Norman and Andrews* v. *Boxes Ltd.*[10] and *Milner* v. *H. Hague Sharp & Co.*[11] The Government has already announced its intention to amend the scheme so that both men and women can claim redundancy payments until the age of 65 and it is to be hoped that similar action will be taken in connection with the statutory sick pay scheme. In the meantime employers are in the extraordinary position of discriminating by applying a statutory provision.

---

[9] C.O.I.T. 00083/88.
[10] C.O.I.T. 21360/87.
[11] C.O.I.T. 2470/88.

EEC LEGISLATION

Enforceability of EEC Directives

11.15   It is important to note when assessing the impact of EEC law on United Kingdom employees, that whereas Article 119 has both vertical and horizontal effect, directives have only vertical effect. The result of this is that whilst Article 119 can be applied directly not only against the State and State employers, but also against private employers, directives create a right which is enforceable by an individual only against the State or State authority. This leads to two important results. First, those employed by State bodies will have greater rights than those with private employers. For example, Mrs. Marshall in *Marshall* v. *Southampton and South-West Hampshire Area Health Authority*[12] (E.C.J. decision on the main point) was able to complain of unlawful discrimination contrary to the equal treatment directive where at the time she would not have been able to bring a claim under United Kingdom law. She was dismissed at age 62, on grounds that she had passed the normal retirement age for women, in circumstances in which men were entitled to continue to work until 65. Mrs. Duke in *Duke* v. *Reliance Systems*[13] had a similar complaint, but it was barred by virtue of section 6(4) of the Sex Discrimination Act 1975 which excluded complaints of discrimination with respect to provisions "in relation to death or retirement." Although *Marshall* made it clear that what occurred was a breach of the equal treatment directive, there was no independent right based on that directive, and therefore a private employer, unlike a State employer, could rely upon the exclusion in section 6(4).

Compensation and the Distinction Between State and Private Employers

11.16   The second, and perhaps more significant effect of the distinction between State and private employers, and one which survives the Sex Discrimination Act 1986, arose when Mrs. Marshall's application was remitted to the Industrial Tribunal to consider the question of remedy. Rather surprisingly, the tribunal held that, despite the domestic statutory limit on compensation, the applicant was entitled to the full total of the loss arising out of her dismissal being £19,405.

---

[12] [1986] I.R.L.R. 140.
[13] [1987] I.C.R. 449.

Their reasoning was as follows.   **11.17**

(a) The statutory limit on compensation was originally calculated as a multiple of 'a week's pay.' However, although the limit on a week's pay has been reviewed annually, the limit on compensation has not kept in step. If it had it would now stand at around £17,000.

(b) In the *Van Colson*[14] case the European Court held that "if a Member State chooses to penalise breaches by the award of compensation, then in order to ensure that it is effective and that it has a deterrent effect that compensation must be adequate in relation to the damage sustained." £8,500 is not a deterrent to any, save a very small, employer.

(c) The Government was in breach of Article 6 which requires all Member States to introduce into their national legal systems "such measures as are necessary to enable all persons who consider themselves wronged . . . to pursue their claims by judicial process." As construed in *Van Colson*, that judicial process must include an adequate remedy. As the remedy provided under section 65 of the Sex Discrimination Act 1975 is not adequate, there must, of necessity, be a breach of Article 6.

The applicant, as an employee of what is, in effect, part of the State, **11.18** was entitled to rely upon Article 6 in a complaint before the Industrial Tribunal. The Tribunal then went on to award the applicant £19,405 and said that to do otherwise would permit the respondent as an emanation of the State to escape liability for £13,155 by reason of the State's own failure to comply with the directive.

It is interesting to compare Mrs. Marshall's case with that of Mrs. Nicol **11.19** who was employed by the Ben Line Group Ltd., and not by an emanation of the State. The normal retirement ages for Ben Line's employees were originally 60 for women and 65 for men. These were also the ages at which their pensions became payable under the company's pension scheme. The company decided to reduce the retirement and pensionable age of its male employees to 60. It realised that after the reduction in retirement age, male employees would receive lower benefits under the pension scheme because of their shorter service, and would not be entitled to a State pension until they were 65. The company therefore made transitional arrangements for existing male employees which allowed them to work for various periods beyond the age of 60, in order to give them time to adjust to and plan for their earlier retirement.

---

[14] [1984] E.C.R. 1891.

EEC LEGISLATION

11.20   Mrs. Nicol notified the company that she wished to work on beyond the age of 60. The company refused her request and required her to retire on her 60th birthday. She complained to an Industrial Tribunal which found that the transitional arrangements were clearly discriminatory, since they applied to male employees only, and concluded that she had been both unlawfully discriminated against and unfairly dismissed. The Tribunal accepted Mrs. Nicol's evidence that her age made it unlikely that she would find another job, and awarded her the maximum of £8,500 towards her loss of earnings. However her actual loss of earnings from having to retire five years earlier than a male colleague would have amounted to £26,760. Had she been employed by a State employer, she might have argued that the statutory limit on the compensation awardable should be disregarded as being in breach of the equal treatment directive.

11.21   The cases show that certain provisions of EEC law can be directly enforceable in the United Kingdom. If the words of a United Kingdom statute are quite clear, and it is impossible to reconcile those words with a provision of EEC law which is directly enforceable, how will the EEC law have direct effect? There are two possibilities:

(a) the EEC provision establishes a 'free-standing' right, running alongside the United Kingdom statute, which can be relied on in preference to it;

(b) the EEC law provision has the effect of amending the words and meaning of the inconsistent statute.

11.22   The problem arose in the case of *Pickstone* v. *Freemans*.[15] As the United Kingdom statute was unambiguous none of the judges in the Court of Appeal felt it appropriate to refer the matter to the E.C.J. One judge wished to make the Equal Pay Act conform with Community law by inserting words to make it consistent with Article 119, but the other two judges thought that Mrs. Pickstone should be able to rely directly on Article 119. This being the majority view it seems that, in cases of blatant inconsistency, directly effective EEC law would be made to prevail over United Kingdom law, by means of free-standing rights, enforceable by individuals who would otherwise be denied the benefit of those rights. Note however, Lord Justice Oliver's approach in *Litster* v. *Forth Engineering*[16] (see 9.13 above) in which he preferred the notional addition of words to the domestic legislation. It may depend perhaps on which came first—the U.K. or EEC legislation.

---

[15] [1987] I.C.R. 867.
[16] [1989] 2 W.L.R. 634.

Jurisdiction

A subsidiary issue arises from this: if an individual has a 'free-**11.23** standing' Community right to assert in the employment field, separate from his contracted rights, does he complain to the Industrial Tribunal or to the Court? Originally, a strict view was taken that as the Industrial and Employment Appeal Tribunals were statutory bodies they had no jurisdiction except that conferred on them by statute. No statute had expressly given them a European jurisdiction and so they had none.[17]

Lord Denning thought otherwise, and said so both in *Shields* v. **11.24** *Coomes Holdings*[18] and in the *Worringham* case (see above). Concern has been expressed as to whether or not, by virtue of the European Communities Act 1972, Parliament can be taken to have conferred European jurisdiction on the Courts and Tribunals. However, the learned editor of Harvey states that the matter has been resolved and, it is submitted, the cases support this view. The House of Lords has implicitly confirmed that the E.A.T. (and therefore presumably the Industrial Tribunal) has European jurisdiction, as in *Garland* v. *British Rail*[19] it said that the E.A.T. was wrong to construe the Sex Discrimination Act 1975 in isolation and should have taken account of European legislation on the subject. In *Pickstone* v. *Freemans*[20] the Court of Appeal ordered the case to be remitted to the Industrial Tribunal for a hearing confined to Mrs. Pickstone's claim under Article 119, and this would seem to put the point beyond doubt.

So far as the Industrial Tribunal jurisdiction in the United Kingdom is **11.25** concerned, section 128 of E.P.C.A. provides that the Secretary of State may, by regulations, make provision for the establishment of tribunals to be known as Industrial Tribunals "to exercise the jurisdiction conferred on them by, or under, this Act or any other Act, whether passed, before or after this Act." It is submitted that it is a matter for argument as to whether or not the European Communities Act 1972 conferred on Industrial Tribunals a jurisdiction to deal with any Article that may be deemed, subsequent to the 1972 Act, to be directly effective in relation to United Kingdom law. There is certainly no reference in the Industrial Tribunals (Rules of Procedure) Regulations which throws any light on the point.

---

[17] See *Snoxell and Davies* v. *Vauxhall Motors Ltd.* [1977] I.C.R. 700.
[18] [1978] I.C.R. 1159.
[19] [1983] 2 A.C. 751.
[20] [1987] I.C.R. 867.

EEC Law and Future Trends

11.26   It cannot be stressed too strongly that the future of the law affecting contracts of employment in the United Kingdom, in particular in relation to equal pay, will be very substantially influenced by European developments. A reference back to the passages on the Protection of Employment (Transfer of Undertakings) Regulations 1981 (see Chap. 9 para. 9.13) and the recent cases of *P. Bork International A.S.* v. *Foreningen AF Arbeljdsledere I Damansk*,[21] and *Litster* v. *Forth Estuary Engineering Ltd.*[22] will serve to show that in that area also domestic law is being influenced quite dramatically by developments in Europe and that the House of Lords are willing to construe United Kingdom legislation 'purposively' in the light of European directives. Practitioners will need to take great care to track these developments in Europe as well as developments on the domestic front.

---

[21] [1989] I.R.L.R. 41, E.C.J.
[22] See n.16 above.

CHAPTER 12

IMMIGRATION

As a general rule, no 'foreign national' may take employment, and thus **12.1** lawfully enter into a contract of employment, in the United Kingdom without authorisation in advance from the Department of Employment and the Home Office. See below for rules affecting EEC and Commonwealth nationals.

The principles of United Kingdom immigration law are laid down in the **12.2** Immigration Act of 1971 as amended. Specific immigration categories, qualifications and conditions are to be found in the Immigration Rules (HC169 as amended) which are subject to frequent amendment. Officers of the Home Office and the Department of Employment have considerable discretion. There is a system of internal administrative review within the Department of Employment and a statutory right of appeal against Home Office decisions.

Conditions for the Granting of Work Permits

Authorisation normally takes the form of a work permit. In addition **12.3** visas are also mandatory for a number of Asian and African nationals and holders of East European passports. The United Kingdom employer must obtain a work permit from the Department of Employment before the prospective employee arrives in the United Kingdom. Permits will only be issued for a limited period (subject to extension) and for a specific vacancy and are subject to the following strict criteria:

(a) The job requires professional qualifications, senior executive experience or unusual technical qualifications.

    (b) The employer has advertised the vacancy in the national press and in any appropriate professional journals and no United Kingdom or EEC candidate with the necessary qualifications has been identified.

    (c) The prospective employee is aged between 23 and 54 and has previous work experience in his field which he has gained overseas.

12.4 The advertising requirement is waived for an inter-company transfer where the employee has worked for a foreign parent or associated company prior to his transfer to the United Kingdom.

12.5 A work permit holder may be accompanied by his wife and children under 18 and his wife may work in the United Kingdom without a work permit. However a woman work permit holder may not as yet be accompanied by her husband unless he can obtain a separate immigration status in his own right. In all cases the family of work permit holders must obtain advance entry clearance from the British Embassy or Consulate in their home country before entering the United Kingdom, and non-EEC and non-Commonwealth nationals must normally register with the police on arrival. After four years' continuous employment, a work permit holder and his family may be eligible for settled residential status, following which all restrictions on length of stay and employment will be removed.

12.6 Special temporary work permits are issued for periods of training and work experience in the United Kingdom up to a maximum of two years. Holders must be between 18 and 35 years old, be at the start of their careers, and the post must be surplus to the employer's normal staffing requirements. At the end of the period the trainee must leave the United Kingdom and is not eligible for a full work permit.

EEC Citizens

12.7 EEC citizens are entitled to work in the United Kingdom without a work permit under EEC Freedom of Movement Regulations. These provisions cover nationals of France, Ireland, Germany, Belgium, Italy, Holland, Luxembourg and Greece at present and will eventually be extended to Spanish and Portuguese citizens. An EEC citizen is given six months' initial leave on arrival and may subsequently be issued with a five-year EEC residential permit.

12.8 Commonwealth citizens with a parent born in the United Kingdom may freely enter and work without restriction. Commonwealth citizens who have one United Kingdom-born grandparent may work in the United Kingdom without work permits but they must obtain advance entry clearance and on arrival are given settled status.

Permit-free Employment

12.9 There are special provisions governing certain categories of permit-free employment, the immigration status of a representative of an overseas company which has not yet established a United Kingdom office or branch, and the admission of self-employed businessmen. Anyone who enters the United Kingdom as a visitor is expressly prohibited from taking employment and to do so is a criminal offence. A visitor may however 'transact business' in the United Kingdom and the distinction between business and employment remains something of a grey area. In principle the definition includes negotiation and signing of contracts, attending business meetings, advising, counselling and training local staff, setting up or developing management and computer systems, and providing managerial, technical and financial assistance.

Dismissal of Illegal Workers

12.10 To terminate a contract of employment and dismiss someone because they do not have the necessary permission is prima facie capable of being fair under section 57(2)(*d*) of E.P.C.A. Note, however, the case of *Bouchaala* v. *Trusthouse Forte Hotels Ltd.*[1] Bouchaala was a trainee manager from Tunisia. He had a permit for his studies, and at the end of such studies the Department of Employment told Trusthouse Forte that continuing to employ him would be illegal and he was dismissed. Later the Home Office said he did not need a work permit. The tribunal found that the reason for dismissal was "statutory ban" and that the employer's genuine but incorrect view that his continued employment was illegal sufficed. The E.A.T. found it very difficult and concluded the genuine belief did not bring the matter within section 57(2)(*d*) but that it could amount to "some other substantial reason." This does raise the illegality issue. It is submitted that a contract with someone who does not have the relevant status or permission is an illegal contract from the beginning. The consequence is that it is unenforceable and that no contractual or statutory rights can be claimed under it.

---

[1] [1980] I.C.R. 721.

APPENDICES

1. Particulars S.1

2. Application form

3. Reference to Company Doctor

4. Check list for contract of employment

5. Worked tax example

6. Amounts of statutory maternity pay

7. Guidelines for maternity policy

8. Checklist for S.S.P. contract provisions and amounts of S.S.P.

9. Transfer of Undertakings (Protection of Employment) Regulations 1981

Appendix 1

Requirements of the Employment Protection (Consolidation) Act 1978

Section	Requirement
1(1)	Provide a written statement within 13 weeks in accordance with the Act
1(2)(*a*)	Identify parties
1(2)(*b*)	Date of commencement
1(2)(*c*)	State whether any previous employment counts and, if so, when it began
1(3)(*a*)	Scale and rate of remuneration
1(3)(*b*)	Intervals of payment
1(3)(*c*)	Any terms as to hours of work and normal working hours
1(3)(*c*)(i)	Holidays and holiday pay, (and accrued entitlement on termination, if any)
1(3)(*c*)(ii)	Sickness and sick pay
1(3)(*c*)(iii)	Pension scheme
1(3)(*e*)	Notice to be given or received
1(3)(*f*)	Title of job
4(a)	Any disciplinary rules of reference to a relevant document

APPENDIX 1

4(b)(i)	Specify any person to whom the employee can apply if dissatisfied with any disciplinary decision and the manner in which such application should be made
4(b)(ii)	Specify any person to whom the employee can apply to redress any grievance and the manner in which such application should be made
4(c)	Explanation of grievance procedure
4(d)	Whether a contracting-out certificate is in force

(N.B. Ss.4(a), (b), and (c) do not apply to Health & Safety rules)

Specimen Job Application Form

Confidential   **Please complete and return to:**

Job applied for:

Personal Details

Surname: First Names:
Home Address: Private telephone No.

                                    Other daily contact
                                    number if appropriate:

Age: Date of birth: Country of Birth: Nationality:

Marital Status: Number of dependent children and their
                         ages:

Ethnic origin; please specify: [here consider specifying the
                                 C.R.E. recommended categories
                                 for applicant to select]

Medical History

Please give brief details and dates of any serious illnesses operations and disabilities.

Are you a registered disabled person?

If so, please quote your registration number:

Please state whether you have been convicted of any criminal offence within the last five years and if so, what?

Name and address of next of kin:

Telephone no.   Home:
                                 Office:

Education
Dates   Names of secondary   Examinations
from   to   Schools & Colleges   Taken & results
                      attended   obtained

Knowledge of Foreign Languages (state Good, Fair or Slight)

Language   Read   Write   Speak

Technical or other qualifications

Employment History

Please give details here of all positions held within the last five years.
Start with your present or most recent position and work back

Dates from to	Name of employer, address Nature of business	position and duties	Present/ most recent salary	Reason for leaving

Main Outside Activities and Interests

Please state what period of notice you have to give in your present job

When would you be available to commence employment?

How did you hear of this vacancy?

Referees—Names and Addresses of Two Referees

(References will not be taken up without your permission)

Medical Arrangements [here set out what is required of the applicant]

Declaration

The facts and matters set out in this application for employment are to
the best of my knowledge, true and complete.
Signature of applicant .Date . . . .

APPENDIX 2

Checklist for Employer—Not on Form

Interviewed by: .... .Date ....

JOB OFFER/REJECT/FURTHER INTERVIEW

OFFER LETTER SENT:

START DATE:

SALARY:

UNION CHECK-OFF:

PROBATIONARY PERIOD:

MEDICAL RESULT:

REFERENCES TAKEN UP:

REFERENCES SATIFACTORY:

SHIFT, IF ANY

REVIEW DUE:

PENSION POSITION:

CONTRACT SIGNED:

APPENDIX 3

Reference to Company Doctor

Name:

Address:

Age:

The company wishes to apply to your doctor or his deputy and a Consultant/Specialist that you may have seen ("your doctor") for a medical report.
You have the following rights under the Medical Reports Act:

(a) not to consent to any application being made to your doctor;
(b) to ask for sight of any report before disclosure to the company;
(c) to be told when an application for a report is being made;
(d) to stop it being shown to the company or to ask for it to be changed (if you see the report). If the changes are not made and the report is disclosed you have the right to add to it a note of your own;
(e) to ask for a sight of any medical report relating to you supplied by your doctor for employment or insurance purposes in the previous six months. This request should be made direct to your doctor.

There are limited circumstances in which your doctor may refuse to disclose the report to you, *e.g.* where it would reveal information relating to another individual.

Should you wish to ask to see a report, you should ask your doctor within 21 days of the date of this form. If you do not, then your doctor may disclose the report in any event.

If you do not ask to see the report on this form, you are entitled to change your mind and provided you notify your doctor before the report is supplied, then your doctor cannot supply it until either:

(a) 21 days have passed without you arranging access to the report; or

(b) you have consented to the disclosure (if you do arrange access within 21 days)

Please indicate below what you wish to do:
I consent/do not consent to disclosure of my medical history to the company.
I do/do not wish to see any report before it is provided to the company.
I confirm this complies with my rights under the Access to Medical Reports Act 1988.

Signed . . . . .Date . . . .

Your Doctor's name: . . . .

Address:. . . . .

. . . .

Consultant/specialist:. . . . .

. . . .

. . . .

Hospital number: . . . .

APPENDIX 4

Check List for a Contract of Employment

This is not a draft contract but a reminder of certain key points that need to be considered and in respect of which advice may be needed. In some cases each individual's circumstances need to be specifically considered, *e.g.* restrictive covenants, in some cases a standard formula will suffice.

PARTIES

(1) . . . . .of . . . .

. . . .("the Company")

(2) . . . . .of . . . .

. . . .("the Employee")

THE PARTIES AGREE as follows:

1. Job Title and Term/Notice

1.1 The Company shall employ the Employee and the Employee shall serve the Company with effect from the [   ] day of [   ] as [capacity/ies] [for a period of [   ] years from the date hereof] [subject to termination during such period as is hereinafter provided].

1.2 The contract may be terminated by either party giving notice [in writing] to the other [length].

177

1.3 The Company shall be entitled lawfully to terminate the Employee's employment by paying the Employee his salary in lieu of any period of notice required to be given by the Employee to the Company or by the Company to the Employee.

2. Duties

During his employment hereunder the Employee shall:

2.1 perform the duties . . . [Perhaps also duties for any Associated Company (as herein defined)];

2.2 devote the whole of his time, attention and ability to his duties hereunder at such place or places as the Company shall determine;

2.3 comply with all reasonable requests and instructions . . . ;

2.4 faithfully and loyally serve the Company to the best of his ability . . . ;

2.5 not engage in any activities which would detract from the proper performance of his duties hereunder, . . . [external shareholdings].

3. Salary

The Company shall pay to the Employee:

3.1 A salary at the rate of [£   ] per annum (which shall be deemed to accrue from day to day) payable in [arrears] by equal monthly instalments on the [last] day of each month.

3.2 Review.

4. Bonus

An annual bonus may be paid [discretion] [amount] [date for payment] [only paid if still in employment].

5. Pension [plus perhaps Insurance Benefits *viz.* PHI, *etc.*]

The Employee is/will become on [   ] a member of the [   ]
Pension Scheme ('the Scheme') which is/is not contracted out. The
scheme is/is not contributory. [Pension booklet or explanatory notes.]

6. Holidays and holiday pay

6.1   In addition to the normal Bank and Public Holidays the Employee
shall be entitled to [   ] working days' paid holiday during
each [calendar] [holiday] year . . . [carry forward].

6.2   [Proportional entitlement for part year service].

7. Sickness/Incapacity

7.1   [Notification obligation and certificate production].

7.2   [Sick pay] [amount, duration and interaction with S.S.P.].

8. Confidentiality and the Company's Property

The Employee shall not whether before or after termination of his
employment with the Company (for whatever reason) except in the
proper course of the duties of his employment or as authorised in writing
by the Company or as ordered so to do by a Court of competent
jurisdiction use or disclose [here set out detailed restriction].

9. Inventions

[Details of employee rights and obligations].

10. Copyright and Registered Designs

[Details of employee rights and obligations].

11. Restrictive Covenants

[Great care needs to be taken to tailor these restrictions to the particular needs of the company, its interests and the particular employee's role if these restrictions are to be express conditions of the employee's employment with the company].

12. No claim in respect of termination by reason of corporate reconstruction or amalgamation if offered job with a new company

Golden Parachute (if any).

13. Termination of Directorship

If the Employee ceases to be a director of the Company [or any Associated Company] then his employment hereunder shall automatically terminate [and if this contract terminates the Employee will resign his directorship(s) on the effective date of termination].

14. Termination on the happening of certain events (? Senior employees only)

The Company without prejudice to any remedy which it may have against the Employee for the breach or non-performance of any of the provisions of this Agreement may by notice in writing to the Employee forthwith determine this Agreement if the Employee shall:

14.1 become bankrupt or make any composition or enter into any deed of arrangement with his creditors; or

14.2 become a patient as defined in the Mental Health Act 1983; or

14.3 be convicted of any criminal offence including a serious offence under road traffic legislation in the United Kingdom or elsewhere; or

14.4 commit any act of dishonesty whether relating to the Company, any Associated Company, other employees or otherwise; or

14.5 be prevented by illness or otherwise from performing his duties hereunder for a consecutive period of [   ] months or for an aggregate period of [   ] calendar months in any period of [   ] calendar months; or

14.7 be guilty of any serious misconduct, any conduct tending to bring the company or any Associated Company or any parent or holding company or himself into disrepute, any material breach or non-observance of any of the provisions of this Agreement or neglect fail or refuse to carry out duties properly assigned to him hereunder.]

15. Obligations upon termination of employment

E.g. delivery up of papers, car, credit cards, keys, *etc.*

16. Effect of termination of this Agreement

The expiry or termination of this Agreement howsoever arising shall not operate to affect any of the provisions hereof which are expressed to operate or have effect thereafter and shall not prejudice the exercise of any right or remedy of either party accrued beforehand.

17. Waiver of rights under E.P.C.A.

[The Employee agrees that he shall not be entitled to make any claim for a redundancy payment or for any compensation for unfair dismissal pursuant to the Employment Protection (Consolidation) Act 1978 or any statutory re-enactment of the relevant provisions thereof by virtue of the expiry of the term of employment hereunder without its being renewed.]

[*N.B.* subject to length of term]

18. Other terms and conditions

18.1 The provisions of the Company's standard terms and conditions of employment and the rule book of the Company as they may be amended from time to time [shall be terms of the Employee's employment hereunder except so far as they are inconsistent with this Agreement.]

18.2 The following particulars are given in compliance with the requirements of section 1 of the Employment Protection (Consolidation) Act, 1978.

    18.2.1 The employment of the Employee by the Company began on [19   ]. [see paragraph 1.1].

    18.2.2 No employment of the Employee with a previous employer counts as part of the Employee's continuous employment with the Company [and his period of continuous employment began on [   ] 19[   ]].

    18.2.3 The Employee's hours of work shall be [the normal hours of work of the Company which are from [   ] a.m. to [   ] p.m.] [together with such additional hours . . .] [overtime].

    18.2.4 If the Employee is dissatisfied with any disciplinary decision or if he has any grievance relating to his employment hereunder he should . . . [outline steps to be taken].

    [18.2.5 No Contracting-out Certificate pursuant to the provisions of the Social Security Pensions Act 1975 is in force in respect of the Employee's employment hereunder.]

    18.2.6 Save as otherwise herein provided there are no terms or conditions of employment relating to hours of work or to normal working hours or to entitlement to holiday (including Public Holidays) or holiday pay or to incapacity for work due to sickness or injury or to pensions or pension schemes.

19. Notices

Any notice to be given hereunder shall be in writing. Notice to the Employee shall be sufficiently served by being delivered personally to him or by being sent by first class post addressed to him at his usual or last known place of abode. Notice to the Company shall be sufficiently served by being delivered to [   ] (or in his absence his nominee) or by being sent by first class post to the registered office of the Company. Any notice if so posted shall be deemed served upon the third day following that on which it was posted.

20. Definition of Associated Company

In this Agreement an 'Associated Company' means any company which for the time being is:

20.1 A holding company (as defined by section 736 of the Companies Act 1985) of the Company; or

20.2 Any subsidiary (as defined by section 736 of the Companies Act 1985) of any such holding company or of the Company; or

[N.B. check the Companies Act 1989 for changed definition; this was not enacted at the time of going to print]

20.3 A company over which the Company has control within the meaning of section 840 of the Income and Corporation Taxes Act 1988.

21. Applicable law

English law shall apply to this Agreement and the parties submit to the jurisdiction of the English Courts.

AS WITNESS the hands of the parties the day and year first above written

SIGNED by   )
)
for and on behalf of   )
Company in the presence of:)

SIGNED by   )
)
in the presence of:)

Appendix 5

Calculation of Net Damages

Damages for 18 months

Value of gross benefits

Salary p.a.		40,339.00
Health Insurance	1,500.00	
Life Assurance	1,500.00	
Car (obtain AA values)	<u>4,500.00</u>	<u>7,500.00</u>
		47,839.00

Taxable value of salary and benefits

Salary p.a.	40,339	
Car	1,100	
Health Insurance	400	41,839.00

Deduct

Married Man's Allowance	4,375.00	
M.I.R.A.S. (say 10 per cent on £7500)	<u>750.00</u>	<u>5,125.00</u>
Taxable salary		36,714.00

Tax thereon

	Tax	
25 per cent. 1–20,700	5,175.00	
40 per cent. 20701–714	<u>6,405.20</u>	11,580.20
	11,580.20	
N.I.C. (£23.61 per week)		<u>1,227.72</u>

APPENDIX 5

(assume contracted out)

<u>Total tax and NIC payable</u>	12,807.92
<u>Gross salary and benefits</u>	47,839.00
Less	
Tax and N.I.C.	<u>12,807.92</u>
Net annual salary and benefits:	35,031.08

Damages

Net annual loss is therefore £35,031.08. Notice period is 18 months therefore multiply £35,031.02 × 1.5 = £52,546.62.

Mitigation

Assume alternative employment is found on the same salary and benefits after 12 months. The net loss is therefore reduced to £35,031.08.
[Alternatively, assume a deduction for mitigation, say 8 per cent. £52,546.62 × 92 per cent. = £48,342.89.]

Accelerated receipt

The above figure should be reduced for accelerated receipt at, say, 8 per cent. £35,031.08 × 92 per cent. = £32,228.59.
[Alternatively £48,342.89 × 92 per cent. = £44,475.46]

Grossing up—Shove v. Downs Surgical plc[1]

Deduct £30,000 to give taxable slice £32,228.59–£30,000 =	£2,228.59
Assume A will pay tax at 40 per cent. on payment as other income received in tax year	
Taxable slice to be grossed up (/0.6)	£3,714.32

[1] [1984] I.C.R. 532

186

to provide sum (+£30,000) A will need to
give him £32,228.59 net of tax

Payment = £30,000 + 3,714.32 =   33,714.32
to give A net of tax (£32,228.59)
A pays 40 per cent. tax on the excess over £30,000, *i.e.* £3,714.32. This
will leave him with £32,228.59 which is the 18 months loss figure less
mitigation and accelerated receipt discount.

[Alternatively

Deduct £30,000 to give
taxable slice £44,475.46–£30,000 =   £14,475.46

Assume A will pay tax at 40 per cent. on payment
as other income received in tax year

Taxable slice to be grossed up (/0.6)   £24,125.77
to provide sum (+£30,000) A will need to
give him £44,475.46 net of tax

Payment = £30,000 + 24,125.77 =   £54,125.77
to give A net of tax (£44,475.46)

A pays 40 per cent. tax on this excess over £30,000, *i.e.* £24,125.77.
This will leave him with £44,475.46 which is the 18 months loss figure
less percentage discounts for mitigation and accelerated receipt.]

It will be seen that the percentage discount for mitigation alternative
favours the employee.

Appendix 6

Amounts of Statutory Maternity Pay

Higher Rate Statutory Maternity Pay

This is 90 per cent. of an employee's normal weekly earnings. Normal weekly earnings are to be calculated in accordance with regulation 21 of the Statutory Maternity Pay (General) Regulations 1986.

Lower Rate Statutory Maternity Pay

This is a prescribed sum and is liable to be changed annually at the start of the financial year. It is currently (from April 2, 1989) £36.25 (Social Security Benefits Up-Rating Order, 1989 Article 10).

Guidelines for Maternity Policy

1. Statutory Maternity Pay

1.1 Does the employee qualify?

1.2 How much statutory maternity pay is due (higher/lower rate)?

1.3 When does statutory maternity pay commence and when does it finish?

1.4 State maternity benefits—are they applicable?

2. Maternity Leave

2.1 Does the employee qualify?

2.2 Notice to be given.

2.3 Length of maternity leave.

2.4 Postponement of return to work.

2.5 Same job or suitable alternative employment.

2.6   Same terms and conditions.

2.7   Is continuity of employment preserved?

3. Company Policy

Note: It is assumed if there is any variation to the statutory rules these will be dealt with in 1 and 2 above.

3.1   Benefits preserved?

3.2   Part-time or full-time work?

Checklist for S.S.P. Contract Provisions and Amounts of S.S.P.

1. State that the employer and employee are bound by the statutory sick pay legislation. If there is a company occupational scheme state that there is, as well as where its terms can be found.

2. Explain briefly how S.S.P. arises:

    2.1   period of incapacity;

    2.2   the period of entitlement, when it begins and ends;

    2.3   what days are qualifying days; make it clear that there are waiting days before S.S.P. is payable.

    Note: remind employees if there is likely to be any doubt whether or not they are excluded for the purpose of S.S.P.

3. State what the rates of pay are, dates of payment and how they may be offset against any occupational scheme.

4. Notification rules: in particular highlight the consequences of failing to give the correct notification.

5. Evidence of incapacity: self certification and appropriate medical evidence.

6. The occupational scheme.

6.1   It is preferable for the employer to retain the discretion to pay remuneration at rates over and above S.S.P.

6.2   Indicate whether there are any waiting days.

6.3   Stress that to qualify for payment under the occupational scheme the additional notification rules must apply.

7.   Link, if appropriate, with the grievance/disciplinary procedure.

S.S.P. Daily Rate Tables

S.S.P. is the weekly rate divided by the number of qualifying days (Q.D.'s) in the week (which begins with Sunday).

TABLE A—STANDARD RATE S.S.P.

No. of Q.D.'s in Week	Standard Rate £52.10 (Average earnings £84.00 or over per week)						
	1 £	2 £	3 £	4 £	5 £	6 £	7 £
7	7.45	14.89	22.33	29.78	37.22	44.66	52.10
6	8.69	17.37	26.05	34.74	43.42	52.10	
5	10.42	20.84	31.26	41.68	52.10		
4	13.03	26.05	39.08	52.10			
3	17.37	34.74	52.10				
2	26.05	52.10					
1	52.10						

TABLE B—LOWER RATE S.S.P.

No. of Q.D.'s in Week	Standard Rate £36.25 (Average earnings £43.00–£83.99)						
	1 £	2 £	3 £	4 £	5 £	6 £	7 £
7	5.18	10.36	15.54	20.72	25.90	31.08	36.25

6	6.05	12.09	18.13	24.17	30.21	36.25
5	7.25	14.50	21.75	29.00	36.25	
4	9.07	18.13	27.19	36.25		
3	12.09	24.17	36.25			
2	18.13	36.25				
1	36.25					

Practical Example

An employee has average weekly earnings of £175 and the Q.D.'s in the week in respect of which you are to be paying S.S.P. are Monday to Friday. No waiting days have been served and the employee is sick from Monday to Friday.

(a) The average weekly earnings are equal to or more than £84.00 so Table A—Standard Rate S.S.P. is applicable to establish the S.S.P. to be paid.

(b) The first three qualifying days are waiting days and S.S.P. is not payable for those days so S.S.P. is only paid for Thursday and Friday in the week.

(c) There are five qualifying days in the week so now find '5' in the 'Number of Q.D.'s in week' column.

(d) S.S.P. is to be paid for two days so cross-refer to the column headed by '2.' £20.84 is the S.S.P. to be paid.

(e) S.S.P. is subject to P.A.Y.E. and National Insurance deductions.

APPENDIX 9

Transfer of Undertakings (Protection of Employment) Regulations 1981

(S.I. 1981, No. 1794)

A draft of these Regulations has been approved by resolution of each House of Parliament in pursuance of paragraph 2(2) of Schedule 2 to the European Communities Act 1972. They are dated December 14, 1981, and made by the Secretary of State, being a Minister designated for the purposes of section 2(2) of that Act in relation to rights and obligations relating to employers and employees on the transfer or merger of undertakings, businesses or parts of businesses, in exercise of the powers conferred by that section.

Citation, commencement and extent

1.— (1) These Regulations may be cited as the Transfer of Undertakings (Protection of Employment) Regulations 1981.

(2) These Regulations, except Regulations 4 to 9 and 14, shall come into operation on February 1, 1982 and Regulations 4 to 9 and 14 shall come into operation on May 1, 1982.

(3) These Regulations, except Regulations 11(10) and 13(3) and (4), extent to Northern Ireland.

Interpretation

2.— (1) In these Regulations—

"collective agreements," "employers' association," and "trade union" have the same meanings respectively as in the 1974 Act or, in Northern Ireland, the 1976 Order;

"collective bargaining" has the same meaning as it has in the 1975 Act or, in Northern Ireland, the 1976 Order;

"contract of employment" means any agreement between an employee and his employer determining the terms and conditions of his employment;

"employee" means any individual who works for another person whether under a contract of service or apprenticeship or otherwise but does not include anyone who provides services under a contract for services and references to a person's employer shall be construed accordingly;

"the 1974 Act," "the 1975 Act," "the 1978 Act" and "the 1976 Order' mean, respectively, the Trade Union and Labour Relations Act 1974, the Employment Protection Act 1975, the Employment Protection (Consolidation) Act 1978 and the Industrial Relations (Northern Ireland) Order 1976;

"recognised," in relation to a trade union, means recognised to any extent by an employer, or two or more associated employers (within the meaning of the 1978 Act, or, in Northern Ireland, the 1976 Order), for the purpose of collective bargaining;

"relevant transfer" means a transfer to which these Regulations apply and "transferor" and "transferee" shall be construed accordingly; and

"undertaking" includes any trade or business but does not include any undertaking or part of an undertaking which is not in the nature of a commercial venture.

(2) References in these Regulations to the transfer of part of an undertaking are references to a transfer of a part which is being transferred as a business and, accordingly, do not include references to a transfer of a ship without more.

(3) For the purposes of these Regulations the representative of a trade union recognised by an employer is an official or other person authorised to carry on collective bargaining with that employer by that union.

A relevant transfer

3.— (1) Subject to the provisions of these Regulations, these Regulations apply to a transfer from one person to another of an undertaking situated immediately before the transfer in the United Kingdom or a part of one which is so situated.

(2)   Subject as aforesaid, these Regulations so apply whether the transfer is effected by sale or by some other disposition or by operation of law.

(3)   Subject as aforesaid, these Regulations so apply notwithstanding—

(a)   that the transfer is governed or effected by the law of a country or territory outside the United Kingdom;

(b)   that persons employed in the undertaking or part transferred ordinarily work outside the United Kingdom;

(c)   that the employment of any of those persons is governed by any such law.

(4)   It is hereby declared that a transfer of an undertaking or part of one may be effected by a series of two or more transactions between the same parties, but in determining whether or not such a series constitutes a single transfer regard shall be had to the extent to which the undertaking or part was controlled by the transferor and transferee respectively before the last transaction, to the lapse of time between each of the transactions, to the intention of the parties and to all the other circumstances.

(5)   Where, in consequence (whether directly or indirectly) of the transfer of an undertaking or part of one which was situated immediately before the transfer in the United Kingdom, a ship within the meaning of the Merchant Shipping Act 1894 registered in the United Kingdom ceases to be so registered, these Regulations shall not affect the right conferred by section 5 of the Merchant Shipping Act 1970 (right of seamen to be discharged when ship ceases to be registered in the United Kingdom) on a seaman employed in the ship.

Transfers by receivers and liquidators

4.— (1) Where the receiver of the property or part of the property of a company [or the administrator of a company appointed under Part II of the Insolvency Act 1986] or, in the case of a creditor's voluntary winding up, the liquidator of a company transfers the company's undertaking, or part of the company's undertaking (the "relevant undertaking") to a wholly owned subsidiary of the company, the transfer shall for the purposes of these Regulations be deemed not to have been effected until immediately before—

(a) the transferee company ceases (otherwise than by reason of its being wound up) to be a wholly owned subsidiary of the transferor company; or

(b) the relevant undertaking is transferred by the transferee company to another person;

whichever first occurs, and, for the purposes of these Regulations, the transfer of the relevant undertaking shall be taken to have been effected immediately before that date by one transaction only.

(2) In this Regulation—

"creditors' voluntary winding up" has the same meaning as in the Companies Act 1948 or, in Northern Ireland, the Companies Act (Northern Ireland) 1960; and

"wholly owned subsidiary" has the same meaning as it has for the purposes of section 150 of the Companies Act 1948 and section 144 of the Companies Act (Northern Ireland) 1960.

Amendment

The words in square brackets were inserted by the Transfer of Undertakings (Protection of Employment) (Amendment) Regulations 1987 No. 442.

Effect of relevant transfer on contracts of employment, etc.

5.— (1) A relevant transfer shall not operate so as to terminate the contract of employment of any person employed by the transferor in the undertaking or part transferred but any such contract which would otherwise have been terminated by the transfer shall have effect after the transfer as if originally made between the person so employed and the transferee.

(2) Without prejudice to paragraph (1) above, on the completion of a relevant transfer—

(a) all the transferor's rights, powers, duties and liabilities under or in connection with any such contract, shall be transferred by virtue of this Regulation to the transferee; and

(b)   anything done before the transfer is completed by or in relation to the transferor in respect of that contract or a person employed in that undertaking or part shall be deemed to have been done by or in relation to the transferee.

(3)   Any references in paragraph (1) or (2) above to a person employed in an undertaking or part of one transferred by a relevant transfer is a reference to a person so employed immediately before the transfer, including, whether the transfer is effected by a series of two or more transactions, a person so employed immediately before any of those transactions.

(4)   Paragraph (2) above shall not transfer or otherwise affect the liabilities of any person to be prosecuted for, convicted of and sentenced for any offence.

(5)   Paragraph (1) above is without prejudice to any right of an employee arising apart from these Regulations to terminate his contract of employment without notice if a substantial change is made in his working conditions to his detriment; but no such right shall arise by reason only that, under that paragraph, the identity of his employer changes unless the employee shows that, in all the circumstances, the change is a significant change and is to his detriment.

Effect of relevant transfer on collective agreements

6.— Where at the time of a relevant transfer there exists a collective agreement made by or on behalf of the transferor with a trade union recognised by the transferor in respect of any employee whose contract of employment is preserved by Regulation 5(1) above, then,—

(a)   without prejudice to section 18 of the 1974 Act or Article 63 of the 1976 Order (collective agreements presumed to be unenforceable in specified circumstances) that agreement, in its application in relation to the employee, shall, after the transfer, have effect as if made by or on behalf of the transferee with that trade union, and accordingly anything done under or in connection with it, in its application as aforesaid, by or in relation to the transferor before the transfer, shall, after the transfer, be deemed to have been done by or in relation to the transferee and

(b)   any order made in respect of that agreement, in its application in relation to the employee, shall, after the transfer, have effect as if the transferee were a party to the agreement.

Exclusion of occupational pension schemes

7.— Regulations 5 and 6 above shall not apply—

(a)   to so much of a contract of employment or collective agreement as relates to an occupational pension scheme within the meaning of the Social Security Pensions Act 1975 or the Social Security Pensions (Northern Ireland) Order 1975; or

(b)   to any rights, powers, duties or liabilities under or in connection with any such contract or subsisting by virtue of any such agreement and relating to such a scheme or otherwise arising in connection with that person's employment and relating to such a scheme.

Dismissal of employee because of relevant transfer

8.— (1) Where either before or after a relevant transfer, any employee of the transferor or transferee is dismissed, that employee shall be treated for the purposes of Part V of the 1978 Act and Articles 20 to 41 of the 1976 Order (unfair dismissal) as unfairly dismissed if the transfer or a reason connected with it is the reason or principal reason for his dismissal.

(2)   Where an economic, technical or organisational reason entailing changes in the workforce of either the transferor or the transferee before or after a relevant transfer is the reason or principal reason for dismissing an employee—

(a)   paragraph (1) above shall not apply to his dismissal; but

(b)   without prejudice to the application of section 57(3) of the 1978 Act or Article 22(10) of the 1976 Order (test of fair dismissal), the dismissal shall for the purposes of section 57(1)(*b*) of that Act and Article 22(1)(*b*) of that Order (substantial reason for dismissal) be regarded as having been for a substantial reason of a kind such as to justify the dismissal of an employee holding the position which that employee held.

(3) The provisions of this Regulation apply whether or not the employee in question is employed in the undertaking or part of the undertaking transferred or to be transferred.

(4) Paragraph (1) above shall not apply in relation to the dismissal of any employee which was required by reason of the application of section 5 of the Aliens Restriction (Amendment) Act 1919 to his employment.

Effect of relevant transfer on trade union recognition

9.— (1) This Regulation applies where after a relevant transfer the undertaking or part of the undertaking transferred maintains an identity distinct from the remainder of the transferee's undertaking.

(2) Where before such a transfer an independent trade union is recognised to any extent by the transferor in respect of employees of any description who in consequence of the transfer become employees of the transferee, then, after the transfer—

   (*a*) the union shall be deemed to have been recognised by the transferee to the same extent in respect of employees of that description so employed; and

   (*b*) any agreement for recognition may be varied or rescinded accordingly.

Duty to inform and consult trade union representatives

10.—(1) In this Regulation and Regulation 11 below "an affected employee" means, in relation to a relevant transfer, any employee of the transferor or the transferee (whether or not employed in the undertaking or the part of the undertaking to be transferred) who may be affected by the transfer or may be affected by measures taken in connection with it; and references to the employer shall be construed accordingly.

(2)   Long enough before a relevant transfer to enable consultations to take place between the employer of any affected employees of a description in respect of which an independent trade union is recognised by him and that union's representatives, the employer shall inform those representatives of—

   (a)   the fact that the relevant transfer is to take place, when, approximately, it is to take place and the reasons for it; and

   (b)   the legal, economic and social implications of the transfer for the affected employees; and

   (c)   the measures which he envisages he will, in connection with the transfer, take in relation to those employees or, if he envisages that no measures will be so taken, that fact; and

   (d)   if the employer is the transferor, the measures which the transferee envisages he will, in connection with the transfer, take in relation to such of those employees as, by virtue of Regulation 5 above, become employees of the transferee after the transfer or, if he envisages that no measures will be so taken, that fact.

(3)   The transferee shall give the transferor such information at such a time as will enable the transferor to perform the duty imposed on him by virtue of paragraph (2)(d) above.

(4)   The information which is to be given to the representatives of a trade union under this Regulation shall be delivered to them, or sent by post to an address notified by them to the employer, or sent by post to the union at the address of his head or main office.

(5)   Where an employer of any affected employees envisages that he will, in connection with the transfer, be taking measures in relation to any such employees of a description in respect of which an independent trade union is recognised by him, he shall enter into consultations with the representatives of that union.

(6)   In the course of those consultations the employer shall—

   (a)   consider any representations made by the trade union representatives; and

   (b)   reply to those representations and, if he rejects any of those representations, state his reasons.

(7)   If in any case there are special circumstances which render it not reasonably practicable for an employer to perform a duty imposed on him by any of the foregoing paragraphs, he shall take all such steps towards performing that duty as are reasonably practicable in the circumstances.

Failure to inform or consult

11.—(1) A complaint that an employer has failed to inform or consult a representative of a trade union in accordance with Regulation 10 above may be presented to an industrial tribunal by that union.

(2)   If on a complaint under paragraph (1) above a question arises whether or not it was reasonably practicable for an employer to perform a particular duty or what steps he took towards performing it, it shall be for him to show—

    (*a*)   that there were special circumstances which rendered it not reasonably practicable for him to perform the duty; and

    (*b*)   that he took all such steps towards its performance as were reasonably practicable in those circumstances.

(3)   On any such complaint against a transferor that he had failed to perform the duty imposed upon him by virtue of paragraph (2)(*d*) or, so far as relating thereto, paragraph (7) of Regulation 10 above, he may not show that it was not reasonably practicable for him to perform the duty in question for the reason that the transferee had failed to give him the requisite information at the requisite time in accordance with Regulation 10(3) above unless he gives the transferee notice of his intention to show that fact; and the giving of the notice shall make the transferee a party to the proceedings.

(4)   Where the tribunal finds a complaint under paragraph (1) above well-founded it shall make a declaration to that effect and may—

    (*a*)   order the employer to pay appropriate compensation to such descriptions of affected employees as may be specified in the award; or

    (*b*)   if the complaint is that the transferor did not perform the duty mentioned in paragraph (3) above and the transferor (after giving due notice) shows the facts so mentioned, order the transferee to pay appropriate compensation to such descriptions of affected employees as may be specified in the award.

(5)   An employee may present a complaint to an industrial tribunal on the ground that he is an employee of a description to which an order under paragraph (4) above relates and that the transferor or the transferee has failed, wholly or in part, to pay him compensation in pursuance of the order.

(6)   Where the tribunal finds a complaint under paragraph (5) above well-founded it shall order the employer to pay the complainant the amount of compensation which it finds is due to him.

(7)   Where an employer, in failing to perform a duty under Regulation 10 above, also fails to comply with the requirements of section 99 of the 1975 Act or Article 49 of the 1976 Order (duty of employer to consult trade union representatives on redundancy)—

        (a)   any compensation awarded to an employee under this Regulation shall go to reduce the amount of remuneration payable to him under a protective award subsequently made under Part IV of that Act or Part IV of that Order and shall also go towards discharging any liability of the employer under, or in respect of a breach of, the contract of employment in respect of a period falling within the protected period under that award; and

        (b)   conversely any remuneration so payable and any payment made to the employee by the employer under, or by way of damages for breach of, that contract in respect of a period falling within the protected period shall go to reduce the amount of any compensation which may be subsequently awarded under this Regulation;

        but this paragraph shall be without prejudice to section 102(3) of that Act and Article 52(3) of that Order (avoidance of duplication of contractual payments and remuneration under protective awards).

(8)   An industrial tribunal shall not consider a complaint under paragraph (1) or (5) above unless it is presented to the tribunal before the end of the period of three months beginning with—

        (a)   the date on which the relevant transfer is completed, in the case of a complaint under paragraph (1);

(*b*)   the date of the tribunal's order under paragraph (4) above, in the case of a complaint under paragraph (5);

or within such further period as the tribunal consider reasonable in a case where it is satisfied that it was not reasonably practicable for the complaint to be presented before the end of the period of three months.

(9)   Section 129 of the 1978 Act (complaint to be sole remedy for breach of relevant rights) and section 133 of that Act (functions of conciliation officer) and Articles 58(2) and 62 of the 1976 Order (which make corresponding provision for Northern Ireland) shall apply to the rights conferred by this Regulation and to proceedings under this Regulation as they apply to the rights conferred by that Act or that Order and the industrial tribunal proceedings mentioned therein.

(10)   An appeal shall lie and shall lie only to the Employment Appeal Tribunal on a question of law arising from any decision of, or arising in any proceedings before, an industrial tribunal under or by virtue of these Regulations and section 13(1) of the Tribunals and Inquiries Act 1971 (appeal from certain tribunals to the High Court) shall not apply in relation to any such proceedings.

(11)   In this Regulation "appropriate compensation" means such sum not exceeding two weeks' pay for the employee in question as the tribunal considers just and equitable having regard to the seriousness of the failure of the employer to comply with his duty.

(12)   Schedule 14 to the 1978 Act or, in Northern Ireland, Schedule 2 to the 1976 Order shall apply for calculating the amount of a week's pay for any employee for the purposes of paragraph (11) above and, for the purposes of that calculation, the calculation date shall be—

(*a*)   in the case of an employee who is dismissed by reason of redundancy (within the meaning of section 81 of the 1978 Act or, in Northern Ireland, section 11 of the Contracts of Employment and Redundancy Payments Act (Northern Ireland) 1965) the date which is the calculation date for the purposes of any entitlement of his to a redundancy payment (within the meaning of that section) or which would be that calculation date if he were so entitled;

(*b*)   in the case of an employee who is dismissed for any other reason, the effective date of termination (within the meaning of section 55 of the 1978 Act or, in Northern Ireland, Article 21 of the 1976 Order) of his contract of employment;

(c)   in any other case, the date of the transfer in question.

Restriction on contracting out

12.   Any provision of any agreement (whether a contract of employment or not) shall be void in so far as it purports to exclude or limit the operation of Regulation 5, 8 or 10 above or to preclude any person from presenting a complaint to an industrial tribunal under Regulation 11 above.

Exclusion of employment abroad or as a dock worker

13.—(1) Regulations 8, 10 and 11 of these Regulations do not apply to employment where under his contract of employment the employee ordinarily works outside the United Kingdom.

(2)   For the purposes of this Regulation a person employed to work on board a ship registered in the United Kingdom shall, unless—

(a)   the employment is wholly outside the United Kingdom, or

(b)   he is not ordinarily resident in the United Kingdom,

be regarded as a person who under his contract ordinarily works in the United Kingdom.

(3)   Nothing in these Regulations applies in relation to any person employed as a registered dock worker unless he is wholly or mainly engaged in work which is not dock work.

(4)   Paragraph (3) above shall be construed as if it were contained in section 145 of the 1978 Act.

Consequential amendments

14.—(1) In section 4(4) of the 1978 Act (written statement to be given to employee on change of his employer), in paragraph (b), the reference to paragraph 17 of Schedule 13 to that Act (continuity of employment where change of employer) shall include a reference to these Regulations.

(2) In section 4(6A) of the Contracts of Employment and Redundancy Payments Act (Northern Ireland) 1965, in paragraph (*b*), the reference to paragraph 10 of Schedule 1 to that Act shall include a reference to these Regulations.

CONTRACTS OF EMPLOYMENT INDEX

CONTRACTS OF EMPLOYMENT INDEX